CHE
YOUR ꞮꞀꓵ

AND
MONEY FACTS

2000–2001

by

GRAHAM M. KITCHEN, F.C.A.

Consultant Editor
BRIAN GILLIGAN, F.C.A., A.T.I.I., T.E.P.
of BDO Stoy Hayward, Chartered Accountants

foulsham
LONDON • NEW YORK • TORONTO • SYDNEY

foulsham

The Publishing House, Bennetts Close,
Cippenham, Slough, Berks, SL1 5AP, England

ISBN 0-572-02551-3

Printed in Great Britain by WBC Book Manufacturers, Bridgend

Contents

CHAPTER		PAGE
1	Budget summary	5
2	How much for you and how much for the tax inspector	11
3	Tax forms and what to do with them	15
4	How to fill in your 2000 tax return	18 to 47
	Supplementary pages:	
	Employment	20
	Share schemes	23
	Self-employment	25
	Partnership	29
	Land and property	30
	Foreign	32
	Trusts, etc	35
	Capital gains	36
	Non-residence, etc.	37
5	Pay, perks and pensions	48
6	Claiming expenses against your income	59
7	Income from property, investments, etc.	62
8	Interest and other payments allowed for tax	66
9	Personal allowances	72
10	Family tax matters	74
11	PAYE and code numbers	81
12	How to check your tax	84
13	Pensioners – your tax and your savings	90
14	Self-employed	99
15	National Insurance	110
16	Capital gains tax	113
17	Inheritance tax	120
18	Money matters	124
	Self assessment – tax calculation working sheets	133
	Working sheets	136
	Personal reminders	138
	Rates of tax and allowances	139
	Working families' and disabled tax credits	140
	Social security benefits	141
	Index	142

CHAPTER ONE

Budget Summary

Although the changes proposed in the March 2000 Budget and pre-Budget report of November 1999 are dealt with throughout this book, this chapter summarises the main points and other relevant legislation, and gives references to the pages which deal specifically with each topic.

Personal allowances

The allowances for 2000–2001 are as follows:

		Page No.
Personal allowances:	£	
age under 65	4,385	72
age 65–74*	5,790	91
age 75 or over*	6,050	91
Married couple's allowance:		
age under 65	Nil	72
age 65 before 6 April 2000*	5,185†	91
age 75 or over*	5,255†	91
minimum amount	2,000†	92
*Income limit	17,000	91
Additional personal allowance	Nil	73
Widow's bereavement allowance	2,000†	73
(only applies to bereavements in 1999–2000)		
Blind person's allowance	1,400	73

† Relief at only 10 per cent.

Rates of tax

In last year's Budget it was announced that the new starting rate of tax of 10 per cent on the first £1,500 of taxable income excluded savings income. However, the pre-Budget report last November announced that it would *include* savings income and this was backdated to 6 April 1999. It also applies to 2000–2001 with the starting rate band increased to £1,520.   139

The basic rate is reduced to 22 per cent from 6 April

2000 with the higher rate of 40 per cent continuing but with the threshold increased to £28,400.

The savings income tax rate (other than for dividends) for basic rate taxpayers remains at 20 per cent for 2000–2001 (after the £1,500 '10 per cent band').

The rates of tax applicable to dividends remain at 10 per cent for income below the basic rate limit and 32.5 per cent above it in 2000–2001. 139

Married couple's allowance and associated allowances
The married couple's allowance is withdrawn from 6 April 2000 except for those couples where either the husband or wife was aged 65 or more on or before 5 April 2000.

The widow's bereavement allowance and additional personal allowance are also withdrawn from 6 April 2000 except for a woman widowed in 1999–2,000, when the widow's bereavement allowance is £2,000. 72

Maintenance payments
The tax relief is abolished from 6 April 2000 except for those couples where either the husband or wife is aged 65 or over on or before 5 April 2000. Payments received will not be taxable in any event from 6 April 2000. 69

Mortgage interest relief
This relief is withdrawn from 6 April 2000.

This relief will no longer be given for loans to provide a life annuity taken out after 9 March 1999, but existing loans will continue to benefit from the relief for the duration of the loan, even if it extends after 5 April 2000. 66

Home income plans
It is confirmed that the interest tax relief will continue for loans in existence on 9 March 1999 at a rate of 22 per cent. 96

Working families and disabled person's tax credit
The allowances payable under the new working families tax credit scheme are increased from June 2000.

From April 2000 tax credits for employees will be paid through the PAYE system with their wages.

This tax credit scheme replaces family credit and disability working allowance. A summary of tax credits available is shown on page 140.   75

Company car benefits
There is no change in the car benefit rates but the fuel scale charges are increased by over 40 per cent from 6 April 2000.

A new basis for calculating company car benefits will start from 6 April 2002 and will be graduated according to the car's carbon dioxide emissions.

The business mileage and age-related discounts will be abolished from that date.   51

Transport benefits
Employees using their own motorcycle for business mileage can claim a tax free mileage allowance of 24p a mile from 6 April 2000.   54

National Insurance contributions (NIC)
There are alterations to the rates and exemptions for 2000–2001. Employers will be liable to pay NIC on most taxable benefits in kind from 6 April 2000, excepting employer's childcare provision.   112

Employee share ownership
Refinements and extensions to the new all-employee share schemes were announced. It was also confirmed that SAYE   57
and company share option plans would not be altered but Approved Profit Sharing Schemes will be abolished in 2002.

Individual learning accounts
Individual learning accounts are replacing Vocational training relief in 2000–2001.   66

Individual Savings Accounts (ISAs)
The subscription limit will be £7,000 for 2000–2001.   126

Gifts of shares to charities
From 6 April 2000 quoted shares and securities can be gifted to charities and the full market value of the gift can be offset against the donor's taxable income.   70

Gift aid
The £250 minimum limit is abolished as from 6 April 2000.   70

Millennium gift aid
Gifts of £100 and over to this gift aid scheme between 31 July 1998 and 31 December 2000 will attract tax relief.   71

Payroll giving
The £1,200 annual maximum limit is abolished from 6 April 2000.

A 10 per cent supplement on payroll giving donations will be added by the Government for three years from April 2000.   130

Pension schemes
The maximum earnings figure is capped at £91,800 as from 6 April 2000.   132

Capital gains tax
A new tax band of 10 per cent for individuals is introduced for 2000–2001.

The annual exemptions limit is increased to £7,200 for 2000–2001 and £3,600 for most Trusts.   114

There are further reliefs for business assets.

Inheritance tax
The tax threshold is increased to £234,000 for deaths on or after 6 April 2000.   122

PAYE payments
The threshold to qualify for quarterly payments is increased from £1,000 to £1,500 a month.   99

Electronic returns
There are discounts for filing PAYE year end returns, VAT and self assessment forms.   99

Capital allowances
The existing first year allowances for plant and machinery in small and medium-sized businesses will be made permanent at the present rate of 40 per cent.   106

A new 100 per cent first year allowance is introduced for small businesses investing in information and communication technology equipment to include computers, software and internet-enabled mobile telephones.

Corporation tax

The full rate for 2000–2001 and 2001–2002 remains at 30 per cent and 20 per cent for small companies with marginal relief where profits fall between £300,001 and £1,500,000. For small companies with taxable profits up to £10,000 the rate will be 10 per cent from 1 April 2000, with marginal relief up to £50,000.   139

VAT

The VAT registration threshold was increased to £52,000, and for de-registration to £50,000.   139

Construction industry scheme

The tax deduction rate for sub-contractors is reduced from 23 per cent to 18 per cent from 6 April 2000.   99

Personal services provided through intermediaries

Although no mention has ever been made of it in any Budget announcements, the Inland Revenue are seeking to treat workers who provide their services via an intermediary, such as a service company and work extensively for one client, as an employee of that client for the purposes of calculating the tax and NIC liability on the income arising from the engagement.   99

Children's tax credit

In 2001–2002 a new tax credit of £442 will be given to families who have one or more children under the age of 16 living with them but it will be scaled down where the person claiming it is liable to tax at the higher rate.

This effectively replaces the married couple's allowance, additional personal allowance, widow's bereavement allowance and relief for maintenance payments which were all abolished from 6 April 2000.   72

Enterprise management incentives

Enables certain companies to grant up to 15 key employees options worth up to £100,000.   128

Enterprise investment scheme and venture capital trusts

There are measures to make these schemes more attractive.   128

Corporate venturing scheme

This scheme is introduced from 1 April 2000 and allows investor companies various tax advantages.   128

Research and development tax credits

Relief is extended from 100 per cent to 150 per cent from 1 April 2000.   106

Stamp duty

As from 28 March 2000 stamp duty was increased to 3 per cent on property costing over £250,000 and to 4 per cent over £500,000.

CHAPTER TWO

How much for you and how much for the tax inspector

Almost everyone receives income in one form or another that is liable to income tax.

You may find, however, that you can avoid paying tax, or reduce your tax bill, either by claiming personal allowances or by offsetting certain types of expenses.

The allowances and expenses you can claim are dealt with later in this book. This chapter tells you what income is free from tax, and what income is taxable.

Taxable income can be divided into two types – earned income and unearned, or investment, income.

The tax inspector can claim part of the following types of 'income':

Earned income
Annuities from past jobs
Benefits – private use of firm's car, petrol, services generally
Benefits of cheap or interest-free loans from your employer for a non-qualifying purpose (see page 55)
Commission, including that from mail order companies, etc.
Compensation for loss of office (but see page 49)
Earnings from casual work and tips
Enterprise allowance
Expense allowances if not spent entirely on firm's business
Holiday pay
Incapacity benefit (except for the first 28 weeks – see also 'tax free' page 13)
Incentive schemes
Income from furnished accommodation (but see page 62)
Income from overseas employment and pensions
Industrial death benefit if paid as a pension
Invalid care allowance
Jobseeker's allowance
Luncheon vouchers – excess over 15p a day per person

Maintenance or alimony (up to 5 April 2000)
Profit related pay (but see page 49)
Profits from trades or professions
Redundancy (see page 49)
Retirement pensions and pensions from a past employer*
Royalties earned from your own work
Salaries, fees and bonuses
State pension*
Statutory maternity pay
Statutory sick pay
Stipends received by clergymen
Wages
Widowed mother's allowance
Widow's pension

*A married woman's retirement pension paid on the basis of her husband's contributions is treated as income of the wife.

Investment income

Annuities purchased
Bank interest
Building society interest
Dividends
Gains from certain non-qualifying insurance policies
Interest
Interest on National Savings Income Bonds and Capital Bonds
Income from overseas investment and property
Income from trusts and from estates of deceased persons
National Savings Bank interest on Investment accounts, but not the first £70 per person on Ordinary accounts
Rents and 'key' money (except holiday lettings) after expenses
Reverse premiums (from 6 April 1999)
Royalties – bought or inherited
Stock or scrip dividends – dividends paid in shares instead of cash

The various rates of tax are shown on page 139.

The following income is all yours – it is free of income tax:
Adoption allowances under approved schemes
Annuities resulting from gallantry awards
Attendance allowance

Awards for damages

Betting, pools and lottery winnings

Car parking benefits

Child benefit and allowances

Christmas bonus for pensioners

Compensation for loss of office, and redundancy pay up to £30,000 (but see page 49)

Compensation for mis-sold personal pensions and personal injury

Disability or Wounds pensions

Disability living allowances (prior to 5 October 1999)

Disabled person's tax credit

Education grants and awards from a local authority or school

Ex-gratia payments up to £30,000 (but see page 49)

Family credit (prior to 5 October 1999)

Family income supplement and family credit

Gifts for employees provided by third parties if under £150 a year

Home improvement, repair and insulation grants

Housing benefit

Incapacity benefit (if previously received as invalidity benefit at 12.4.95 for the same incapacity and first 28 weeks of new claims)

Income support

Individual savings accounts income (ISAs)

Industrial injury benefits

Insurance policy benefits for accident, sickness, disability or unemployment from 6 April 1996 (earlier if linked to mortgage)

Insurance bond withdrawals up to 5 per cent a year but a portion may be subject to tax on redemption

Interest from National Savings Certificates (including index-linked)

Interest on delayed tax repayments

Invalidity pension

Jobfinder's grant

Life assurance policy bonuses and profits

Long-service awards except cash up to £20 for each year of service

Lump sums from an approved pension scheme on retirement

Luncheon vouchers up to 15p per person per day (any cash allowance would be taxable)

Maintenance or alimony (from 6 April 2000)

Maternity allowance

Miners' coal allowance, whether in cash or kind

National Savings Bank interest up to £70 per person on ordinary accounts only

National Savings Certificates increase in value

Pensions from Austria or Germany to victims of Nazi persecution

Personal equity plan dividends reinvested

Premium Bond prizes

Profit-related pay up to £2,000/£1,000 depending on accounting period (see page 49)

Provident benefits up to £4,000 for lump sum payments

Purchased life annuities – the capital proportion of yearly amount

Redundancy (see page 49)

Rent and council tax rebates

Rent-a-room relief up to £4,250 a year (see page 63)

SAYE schemes – interest and bonus

Severe disablement allowance

Shares issued under an approved share incentive scheme, authorised by a tax office, up to a value of £3,000 or, if greater, 10 per cent of the employee's earnings, subject to a maximum of £8,000. After five years the proceeds of sales are tax free.

Share option profits made under the SAYE scheme run by the Department of National Savings – no income tax but capital gains tax may be payable

Sickness benefits under an insurance policy for up to 12 months where the premiums are paid by the employee

Strike and unemployment pay from a trade union

Student grants

Termination payments up to £30,000 (but see page 49)

TESSA interest if kept for the full period

Venture capital trust dividends (but see page 128)

War widow's benefit

Widow's payment (single lump sum)

Winter fuel payment for pensioners

Working families tax credit

CHAPTER THREE

Tax forms and what to do with them

Tax Return

If you receive a tax return you *must* fill it in and return it to your tax office.

There are time limits after which you will be charged penalties and interest (see page 47). Chapter 4 takes you through all aspects of the tax return, and any supplementary forms step by step.

Notice of income tax code P2(T)

Don't just put this in a drawer! Check it as explained on page 81.

Make sure your employer knows of any alteration in your code, and write to your tax office if you disagree with any figure.

Form P60

Your employer has by law to give you this form by 31 May after the end of every tax year. It shows your earnings from that employment and the total PAYE deducted in the year.

Check the form to see if you can claim some tax back as shown on page 84.

Income tax repayment claim (Form R40)

This will be sent to you by your tax office if most of your income has had tax deducted before receipt and you normally have to claim tax back at the end of each tax year although, with the changes in dividend tax credits, there will be fewer such claims.

Enquiry forms
Form 33

This form is issued by the tax office covering your home address or a tax office who knows that you have been paid income by someone in their area. It is important to complete and return it as soon as possible otherwise there could be delays in settling your tax matters in the future.

Form RU6(M)
This is sent to people who have registered with banks or building societies to have their income paid gross – that is without having tax deducted.

Fill in the form carefully, for the tax office send it to you to check your total income to make sure that you are not liable to pay tax (see page 94).

Notice of employee leaving (Form P45)
This form is issued to you by your employer when you leave. If you are immediately going to another job, hand Parts 2 and 3 to your new employer. Otherwise, send them to the tax office shown on the form, together with a letter stating that you are at present unemployed, to see if you can claim a repayment of tax. Keep Part 1A.

If you do not have this form, or if you lose it, then you will have to complete a questionnaire form obtainable from your new employer. He will send this to your tax office and use a temporary code until you either provide a P45 form or the tax office advises him of a new code for you.

Return of expenses and allowances (P11D)
This is an annual form to be completed by an *employer* for staff who receive earnings, expenses and potential benefits of £8,500 a year or more, and for directors. It shows all perks, benefits and expenses that you were paid or given by your employer. (See page 61.)

There is also a Form P9D for employees earning less than £8,500 a year who have received benefits, etc. which are taxable.

Self Assessment – Tax calculation (SA 302)
This notice summarises your income tax situation and shows how much is due or has been overpaid. You must check it carefully and ensure that the figures correspond to those stated in your tax return.

As well as setting out how your tax liability (or refund) is calculated, quite often there will be comments explaining certain figures or responding to queries you have raised.

The calculation will not reflect any payments on account you may have made and you will therefore need to check the calculation with your statement of account to fully confirm your tax position.

It is easy to overlook these comments as the form is prepared on a computer and they don't stand out as they would in a conventional letter, therefore check the form carefully.

If you cannot understand the calculations, or you have a query, telephone the Inland Revenue helpline on 0845 9000 444.

If you cannot submit your return because you have information outstanding, still estimate your tax liability and make payments by the due date to avoid interest and surcharges arising on any amount unpaid.

Self Assessment – Statement of Account (SA 300)

This statement, sent out by your tax office, shows how much tax is due and when it should be paid; it will also show, where applicable, any payments that are due on account.

One of the advantages of the new self assessment tax system is that an individual now only deals with one tax office – in the past, particularly in the case of pensioners or those who have more than one employer, it was possible to deal with two or three tax offices.

General comments

You should not ignore any form or communication from the tax inspector but deal with it immediately, either by replying yourself or passing it on to the tax adviser who deals with your tax affairs.

The deadlines for returning your self assessment tax return are 30 September 2000 (or two months after the date the return form was sent to you, if later) if you want the tax inspector to calculate your tax liability or refund, or 31 January 2001 if you plan to do it yourself.

Interest and penalties for late submission of your tax return or tax payments are now very stringent. (See page 47.)

CHAPTER FOUR

How to fill in your 2000 tax return

Not everyone automatically receives a tax return to fill in every year, but if you do, you *must* complete it and return it to your tax office.

The tax office relies on the fact that it is the taxpayer's responsibility to advise them of any changes in sources of income or claims for expenses and allowances. You may, of course, ask for a tax return to complete if you do not receive one.

A wife is treated as an individual in her own right for tax purposes, getting her own tax return, being responsible for her own tax affairs and getting her own individual tax allowances and exemptions.

The tax year runs from 6 April in one year to 5 April in the following year.

Your tax return for the year ended 5 April 2000 is an eight-page document with dozens of boxes for you to complete; it summarises your income and reliefs and enables you to claim allowances for the year ending 5 April 2000.

Start filling in your tax return by ticking the appropriate boxes on page 2 (reproduced overleaf).

If you answer Yes to any of the questions numbered 1 to 9, then check to see if the tax office have sent you the relevant supplementary pages to complete. If not, then telephone the special order line on 0845 9000 404 and ask for the missing pages. You will need to quote your name, address and tax reference number. Alternatively you can fax on 0845 9000 604.

Blind persons requiring help with a Braille version should telephone 01274 539646.

There is also a website at www.inlandrevenue.gov.uk

The tax return and all the supplementary pages are now reproduced in this book, starting on the next page.

Inland Revenue

INCOME AND CAPITAL GAINS *for the year ended 5 April 2000*

Step 1

Answer Questions 1 to 9 below to find out if you have the right supplementary Pages. Please read pages 6 and 7 of your Tax Return Guide if you need help. The Questions are colour coded to help you identify the supplementary Pages and their guidance notes. If you answer 'No', go to the next question. If you answer 'Yes', you must complete the relevant supplementary Pages. Turn to the back of your Tax Return to see if you have the right ones and look at the back of the Tax Return Guide to see if you have guidance notes to go with them. **Ring the Orderline on 0845 9000 404, or fax on 0845 9000 604 for any you need (open 7 days a week between 8am and 10pm). If I have sent you any Pages you do not need, ignore them.**

Check to make sure you have the right supplementary Pages and then tick the box below.

Q1 Were you an employee, or office holder, or director, or agency worker or did you receive payments or benefits from a former employer (excluding a pension) in the year ended 5 April 2000? | NO | YES | | **EMPLOYMENT YES**

Q2 Did you have any taxable income from share options, shares (but this does not include dividends - they go in Question 10) or share related benefits in the year? | NO | YES | | **SHARE SCHEMES YES**

Q3 Were you self-employed (but not in partnership)? (Tick 'Yes' if you were a Name at Lloyd's.) | NO | YES | | **SELF-EMPLOYMENT YES**

Q4 Were you in partnership? | NO | YES | | **PARTNERSHIP YES**

Q5 Did you receive any rent or other income from land and property in the UK? | NO | YES | | **LAND & PROPERTY YES**

Q6 Did you have any taxable income from overseas pensions or benefits, or from foreign companies or savings institutions, offshore funds or trusts abroad, or from land and property abroad or gains on foreign insurance policies? | NO | YES |

Have you or could you have received, or enjoyed directly or indirectly, or benefited in any way from, income of a foreign entity as a result of a transfer of assets made in this or earlier years? | NO | YES |

Do you want to claim tax credit relief for foreign tax paid on foreign income or gains? | NO | YES | | **FOREIGN YES**

Q7 Did you receive, or are you deemed to have, income from a trust, settlement or deceased person's estate? | NO | YES | | **TRUSTS ETC YES**

Q8 Capital gains
- Have you disposed of your only or main residence? If 'Yes', read page 7 of your Tax Return Guide to see if you need the Capital Gains Pages. | NO | YES |
- Did you dispose of other chargeable assets worth more than £14,200 in total? | NO | YES |
- Were your total chargeable gains more than £7,100? | NO | YES | | **CAPITAL GAINS YES**

  Please see page 7 of the Tax Return Guide if you wish to claim a capital loss.

Q9 Are you claiming that you were not resident, or not ordinarily resident, or not domiciled, in the UK, or dual resident in the UK and another country, for all or part of the year? | NO | YES | | **NON-RESIDENCE ETC YES**

Step 2 **Please use blue or black ink to fill in your Tax Return and please do not include pence. Round down, to the nearest pound, your income and capital gains and round up your tax credits and tax deductions. Now fill in any supplementary Pages BEFORE going to Step 3.**

Tick this box when you have filled in your supplementary Pages. ☐

Step 3 Now fill in Questions 10 to 23. If you answer 'No' to a question, go to the next one. If you answer 'Yes', fill in the relevant boxes.

Remember
- You do not have to calculate your tax - I will do it for you if you send your Tax Return to me by 30 September. This will save you time and effort.
- The Tax Calculation Guide I have sent you will help if you decide to calculate the tax yourself.
- You do not have to wait until 30 September 2000, or 31 January 2001, to send me your Tax Return.

You will see that you will need supplementary pages if you are:

Code sequence		Page in this book
1	In employment	20
2	Participating in share schemes	23
3	Self-employed	25
4	In partnership	29

Code sequence		Page in this book
5	Owning land or buildings	30
6	Receiving foreign income	32
7	Receiving income from trusts or estates	35
8	Declaring capital gains or losses	36
9	Non-resident in the UK	37

Once you are sure you have all the supplementary pages that you need, then the next step is to fill in these *before* you progress through the rest of the tax return.

To summarise:
1. Fill in all the 'Yes'/'No' boxes on page 2 of the main tax return.
2. Fill in the supplementary pages corresponding to the 'Yes' boxes.
3. Fill in the rest of the boxes in the main tax return.

The supplementary pages headed **EMPLOYMENT** cover your income and benefits from employment and your claim for expenses. (There are different versions of this form for Ministers of Religion and Members of Parliament.)

After each section there is a cross-reference to the chapter or page in this book that will give you help in filling in this form.

To fill in these sections you may need copies of your:

P60 or P45 forms	
Notice of code	
P11D form	
Receipts for expenses, etc.	

Inland Revenue

Income for the year ended 5 April 2000

EMPLOYMENT

Fill in these boxes first

Name

Tax reference

If you want help, look up the box numbers in the Notes

Details of employer

Employer's PAYE reference - may be shown under 'Tax Office number and reference' on your P60 or 'PAYE reference' on your P45

1.1

Employer's name

1.2

Date employment started (only if between 6 April 1999 and 5 April 2000)

1.3   /   /

Employer's address

1.5

Date finished (only if between 6 April 1999 and 5 April 2000)

1.4   /   /

Tick box 1.6 if you were a director of the company

1.6

and, if so, tick box 1.7 if it was a close company

1.7

Postcode

Box **1.1** Your employer's PAYE reference should be on the P60 or P45 form

Income from employment	
■ *Money* - see Notes, page EN3	
	Before tax
• Payments from P60 (or P45 or payslips)	**1.8** £
• Payments not on P60 etc. - tips	**1.9** £
- other payments (excluding expenses entered below and lump sums and compensation payments or benefits entered overleaf)	**1.10** £
	Tax deducted
• UK tax deducted from payments in boxes 1.8 to 1.10	**1.11** £

Boxes **1.8** to **1.11** see page 48. You *are* allowed to subtract any deduction made by your employer for contributions to an approved pension scheme or payroll giving donations.

■ *Benefits and expenses* - see Notes, pages EN3 to EN6. If any benefits connected with termination of employment were received, or enjoyed, after that termination and were from a **former** employer you need to complete Help Sheet IR204, available from the Orderline. Do not enter such benefits here.

	Amount			Amount
• Assets transferred/ payments made for you	**1.12** £		• Vans	**1.18** £
• Vouchers/credit cards	**1.13** £		• Interest-free and low-interest loans	**1.19** £
• Living accommodation	**1.14** £		*box 1.20 is not used*	
• Mileage allowance	**1.15** £		• Private medical or dental insurance	**1.21** £
• Company cars	**1.16** £		• Other benefits	**1.22** £
• Fuel for company cars	**1.17** £		• Expenses payments received and balancing charges	**1.23** £

Box no. **1.12**	see page 55	Box no. **1.18**	see page 53
Box no. **1.13**	see page 55	Box no. **1.19**	see page 55
Box no. **1.14**	see page 54	Box no. **1.21**	see page 69
Box no. **1.15**	see page 53	Box no. **1.22**	see page 55
Box no. **1.16**	see page 51	Box no. **1.23**	see page 51
Box no. **1.17**	see page 53		

Income from employment continued

■ *Lump sums and compensation payments or benefits including such payments and benefits from a former employer*
Note that 'lump sums' here includes any contributions which your employer made to an unapproved retirement benefits scheme

You must read page EN6 of the Notes before filling in boxes 1.24 to 1.30

Reliefs

- £30,000 exemption — **1.24** £
- Foreign service and disability — **1.25** £
- Retirement and death lump sums — **1.26** £

Taxable lump sums

- From box H of *Help Sheet IR204* — **1.27** £
- From box Q of *Help Sheet IR204* — **1.28** £
- From box R of *Help Sheet IR204* — **1.29** £
- Tax deducted from payments in boxes 1.27 to 1.29 — Tax deducted **1.30** £

Boxes **1.24** to **1.30** see page 49

■ *Foreign earnings not taxable in the UK in year ended 5 April 2000* - see Notes, page EN6 — **1.31** £

■ *Expenses you incurred in doing your job* - see Notes, pages EN6 to EN8

- Travel and subsistence costs — **1.32** £
- Fixed deductions for expenses — **1.33** £
- Professional fees and subscriptions — **1.34** £
- Other expenses and capital allowances — **1.35** £
- Tick box 1.36 if the figure in box 1.32 includes travel between your home and a permanent workplace — **1.36**

■ *Foreign Earnings Deduction* — **1.37** £

■ *Foreign tax for which tax credit relief not claimed* — **1.38** £

Additional information

Box no. **1.31**	see page 58	Box no. **1.35**	see pages 59 & 106
Box no. **1.32**	see page 60	Box no. **1.36**	see page 60
Box no. **1.33**	see page 59	Box no. **1.37**	see page 58
Box no. **1.34**	see page 60	Box no. **1.38**	see page 58

Where there are several figures to go in one box, use the work sheets provided on pages 136–137 to add them together and thus keep a copy to which you may refer at any time.

The supplementary pages headed **SHARE SCHEMES** cover share options and share related benefits.

To fill in these sections, you may need copies of:

Share option certificates	
Correspondence from your scheme's Trustees	
Market valuations at relevant dates	

You must complete a separate page for each share scheme – you cannot group them together. Telephone the order line on 0845 9000 404 if you want another form. Help sheet IR218 is also available from that number.

As the rules and regulations vary from scheme to scheme, consult your employer or the Trustees of your scheme if you require help or advice before filling in your tax return.

General background information on share schemes is given on page 57.

These supplementary pages only cover any liability to income tax.

If you have made any capital gains or losses on disposing of the shares you may need to declare these in the supplementary pages *Capital Gains* (see pages 36 and 113).

Income for the year ended 5 April 2000

Inland **Revenue**

SHARE SCHEMES

Name   Tax reference

Fill in these boxes first

If you want help, look up the box numbers in the Notes.

Share options

Read the Notes, pages SN1 to SN5 **before** filling in the boxes

■ *Approved savings-related share options*

		Name of company and share scheme	Tick if shares unlisted	Taxable amount
● Exercise	2.1		2.2	2.3 £
● Cancellation or release	2.4		2.5	2.6 £

■ *Approved discretionary share options*

		Name of company and share scheme		
● Exercise	2.7		2.8	2.9 £
● Cancellation or release	2.10		2.11	2.12 £

■ *Unapproved share options*

		Name of company and share scheme		
● Grant	2.13		2.14	2.15 £
● Exercise	2.16		2.17	2.18 £
● Cancellation or release	2.19		2.20	2.21 £

Shares acquired

Read the Notes, page SN6 **before** filling in the boxes

Name of company and share scheme

- Shares acquired from your employment **2.22** **2.23** **2.24** £

- Shares as benefits **2.25** **2.26** **2.27** £

- Post-acquisition charges or lifting of risk of forfeiture **2.28** **2.29** **2.30** £

total column above

- Total of the taxable amounts boxes (boxes 2.3, 2.6, 2.9, 2.12, 2.15, 2.18, 2.21, 2.24, 2.27 and 2.30) **2.31A** £

- Any taxable amounts included in boxes 2.6 to 2.30 which are included in the Pay figure on your P60 or P45(Part 1A) **2.31B** £

box 2.31A *minus* box 2.31B

Total taxable amount **2.31** £

Additional information

Share options

Read the Notes, pages SN2 to SN5 **before** filling in the boxes

Name of company and share scheme **2.32**

Class of share (for example, 10p Ordinary) **2.33**

	Grant	Exercise	Cancellation/Release
2.34 Date option was granted	/ /	/ /	/ /
2.35 Date option was exercised		/ /	
2.36 Number of shares			
2.37 Exercise price/option price per share	£ .	£ .	
2.38 Amount paid for option	£ .	£ .	£ .
2.39 Market value per share at date the option was granted	£ .		
2.40 Market value per share at date the option was exercised		£ .	
2.41 Amount received in money or money's worth			£ .

Shares acquired

Read the Notes, page SN6 **before** filling in the boxes

Name of company and share scheme **2.42**

Class of share (for example, 10p Ordinary) **2.43**

	Shares acquired	Post-acquisition charge
2.44 Date shares acquired or forfeiture lifted	/ /	/ /
2.45 Number of shares		
2.46 Amount paid per share	£ .	
2.47 Market value per share at date of acquisition or forfeiture lifted	£ .	£ .
2.48 Give details of the nature of the post-acquisition event		

The supplementary pages headed **SELF-EMPLOYMENT** cover your business details and a separate sheet needs to be completed for each business. You must fill in these pages if you received income from work done on a self-employed or freelance basis, or you let furnished rooms and provided services so that it was considered as a business – but not if you were in partnership. If you were in partnership, you need the *Partnership* supplementary pages (see page 29), not those for self-employment. There is a different version for Lloyd's Underwriting Names.

If your turnover is less than £15,000 a year, you do not need to fill in page 2 of this form.

Although these supplementary pages appear very complicated at first glance, they are basically requesting the information that should be available from your business accounts but broken down under individual boxes for turnover and expense headings, with separate boxes for capital allowances, adjustments to profits for tax purposes and carrying forward of any losses.

Chapter 14 in this book covers all basic aspects of self-employment.

Income for the year ended 5 April 2000

Inland Revenue

SELF-EMPLOYMENT

Fill in these boxes first

Name

Tax reference

If you want help, look up the box numbers in the Notes

Business details

Name of business

3.1

Description of business

3.2

Address of business

3.3

Postcode

Accounting period - *read the Notes, page SEN2 before filling in these boxes*

Start **3.4** / /

End **3.5** / /

- Tick box 3.5A if you entered details for all relevant accounting periods on last year's Tax Return and boxes 3.11 to 3.70 and 3.93 to 3.109 will be blank *(read Step 3 on page SEN2)* **3.5A**

- Tick box 3.6 if details in boxes 3.1 or 3.3 have changed since your last Tax Return **3.6**

- Tick box 3.7 if your accounts do not cover the period from the last accounting date (explain why in the 'Additional information' box below) **3.7**

- Tick box 3.8A if your accounting date has changed (only if this is a permanent change and you want it to count for tax) **3.8A**

- Tick box 3.8B if this is the second or further change (explain why you have not used the same date as last year in the 'Additional information' box) **3.8B**

- Date of commencement if after 5 April 1996 **3.9** / /

- Date of cessation if before 6 April 2000 **3.10** / /

Additional information

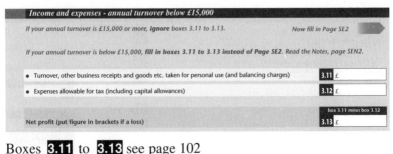

Income and expenses - annual turnover below £15,000

If your annual turnover is £15,000 or more, **ignore** boxes 3.11 to 3.13.   *Now fill in Page SE2*

If your annual turnover is below £15,000, **fill in boxes 3.11 to 3.13 instead of Page SE2**. Read the Notes, page SEN2.

- Turnover, other business receipts and goods etc. taken for personal use (and balancing charges)   **3.11** £

- Expenses allowable for tax (including capital allowances)   **3.12** £

Net profit (put figure in brackets if a loss)   box 3.11 *minus* box 3.12   **3.13** £

Boxes **3.11** to **3.13** see page 102

Income and expenses - annual turnover £15,000 or more

You must fill in this Page if your annual turnover is £15,000 or more - read the Notes, page SEN2

If you were registered for VAT, do the figures in boxes 3.16 to 3.51, include VAT? **3.14**   or exclude VAT? **3.15**   Sales/business income (turnover)   **3.16** £

Disallowable expenses included in boxes 3.33 to 3.50   **Total expenses**

Boxes **3.14** to **3.16** see pages 102–105

• Cost of sales	**3.17** £	**3.33** £
• Construction industry subcontractor costs	**3.18** £	**3.34** £
• Other direct costs	**3.19** £	**3.35** £

box 3.16 *minus* (box 3.33 + box 3.34 + box 3.35)

Gross profit/(loss)   **3.36** £

Other income/profits   **3.37** £

• Employee costs	**3.20** £	**3.38** £
• Premises costs	**3.21** £	**3.39** £
• Repairs	**3.22** £	**3.40** £
• General administrative expenses	**3.23** £	**3.41** £
• Motor expenses	**3.24** £	**3.42** £
• Travel and subsistence	**3.25** £	**3.43** £
• Advertising, promotion and entertainment	**3.26** £	**3.44** £
• Legal and professional costs	**3.27** £	**3.45** £
• Bad debts	**3.28** £	**3.46** £
• Interest	**3.29** £	**3.47** £
• Other finance charges	**3.30** £	**3.48** £
• Depreciation and loss/(profit) on sale	**3.31** £	**3.49** £
• Other expenses	**3.32** £	**3.50** £

Put the total of boxes 3.17 to 3.32 in box 3.53 below

Total expenses   **3.51** £

total of boxes 3.38 to 3.50

boxes 3.36 + 3.37 *minus* box 3.51

Net profit/(loss)   **3.52** £

Boxes **3.17** to **3.52** see pages 102–104

Tax adjustments to net profit or loss

• Disallowable expenses	total of boxes 3.17 to 3.32 **3.53** £	
• Goods etc. taken for personal use and other adjustments (apart from disallowable expenses) that increase profits	**3.54** £	
• Balancing charges	**3.55** £	
Total additions to net profit (deduct from net loss)		boxes 3.53 + 3.54 + 3.55 **3.56** £
• Capital allowances	**3.57** £	
• Deductions from net profit (add to net loss)	**3.58** £	boxes 3.57 + 3.58 **3.59** £
Net business profit for tax purposes (put figure in brackets if a loss)		boxes 3.52 + 3.56 minus box 3.59 **3.60** £

Boxes **3.53** to **3.60** see page 104

Capital allowances - summary

	Capital allowances	Balancing charge
• Motor cars (Separate calculations must be made for each motor car costing more than £12,000 and for cars used partly for private motoring.)	**3.61** £	**3.62** £
• Other business plant and machinery	**3.63** £	**3.64** £
• Agricultural or Industrial Buildings Allowance (A separate calculation must be made for each block of expenditure.)	**3.65** £	**3.66** £
• Other capital allowances claimed (Separate calculations must be made.)	**3.67** £	**3.68** £
Total capital allowances/balancing charges	total of column above **3.69** £	total of column above **3.70** £

Boxes **3.61** to **3.70** see page 104

Adjustments to arrive at taxable profit or loss

Basis period begins **3.71** / / and ends **3.72** / /

• Tick box 3.72A if the figure in box 3.88 is provisional   **3.72A**

• Tick box 3.72B if the special arrangements for certain trades detailed in the guidance notes apply (see Notes, pages SEN8 and SEN10)   **3.72B**

Profit or loss of this account for tax purposes (box 3.13 or 3.60)   **3.73** £

Adjustment to arrive at profit or loss for this basis period   **3.74** £

• Overlap profit brought forward **3.75** £   • Deduct overlap relief used this year **3.76** £

• Overlap profit carried forward **3.77** £

Adjustment for farmers' averaging (see Notes, page SEN8 if you made a loss for 1999-2000)   **3.78** £

Adjustment on change of basis   **3.78A** £

Net profit for 1999-2000 (if loss, enter '0')   **3.79** £

Allowable loss for 1999-2000 (if you made a profit, enter '0')   **3.80** £

• Loss offset against other income for 1999-2000   **3.81** £

• Loss to carry back   **3.82** £

• Loss to carry forward (that is allowable loss not claimed in any other way)   **3.83** £

• Losses brought forward from earlier years   **3.84** £

• Losses brought forward from earlier years used this year   **3.85** £

		box 3.79 minus box 3.85
Taxable profit after losses brought forward		3.86 £
• Any other business income (for example, Business Start-up Allowance received in 1999-2000)		3.87 £
		box 3.86 + box 3.87
Total taxable profits from this business		3.88 £

Chapter 14 will give you background details as to the figures that have to go in boxes 3.71 to 3.88

Class 4 National Insurance Contributions

- Tick this box if exception or deferment applies | 3.89
- Adjustments to profit chargeable to Class 4 National Insurance Contributions | 3.90 £
- Class 4 National Insurance Contributions due | 3.91 £

Subcontractors in the construction industry

- Deductions made by contractors on account of tax (you must send your SC60s/CIS25s to us) | 3.92 £

Summary of balance sheet

Leave these boxes blank if you do not have a balance sheet

■ *Assets*
- Plant, machinery and motor vehicles | 3.93 £
- Other fixed assets (premises, goodwill, investments etc.) | 3.94 £
- Stock and work in progress | 3.95 £
- Debtors/prepayments/other current assets | 3.96 £
- Bank/building society balances | 3.97 £ | total of boxes 3.93 to 3.98
- Cash in hand | 3.98 £ | 3.99 £

■ *Liabilities*
- Trade creditors/accruals | 3.100 £
- Loans and overdrawn bank accounts | 3.101 £ | total of boxes 3.100 to 3.102
- Other liabilities | 3.102 £ | 3.103 £

	box 3.99 minus box 3.103

■ *Net business assets* (put the figure in brackets if you had net business liabilities) | 3.104 £

■ *Represented by*

Capital Account
- Balance at start of period* | 3.105 £
- Net profit/(loss)* | 3.106 £
- Capital introduced | 3.107 £
- Drawings | 3.108 £ | total of boxes 3.105 to 3.107 minus box 3.108
- Balance at end of period* | 3.109 £

* If the Capital Account is overdrawn, or the business made a net loss, show the figure in brackets.

Tax deducted from trading income

- Any tax deducted (excluding deductions made by contractors on account of tax) from trading income. | 3.120 £

Note: box numbers 3.110 to 3.119 are not used

Additional information

Boxes 3.89 to 3.120 see page 111 and Chapter 14.

The **PARTNERSHIP** supplementary pages are not reproduced here in full, as the background information needed to complete them is similar to that covered by the Self-employed section (see page 25) and Chapter 14 covers most of the basic aspects.

There are two types of supplementary pages – Partnership (short) reproduced here and Partnership (long). Use the short version if your only partnership income was trading income or taxed interest from banks, building societies and deposit takers. This will apply to the majority of small partnerships.

Income for the year ended 5 April 2000

Inland Revenue

PARTNERSHIP (SHORT)

Fill in these boxes first

Name	Tax reference

If you want help, look up the box numbers in the Notes

Partnership details

Partnership reference number
4.1

Partnership trade or profession
4.2

- Date you started being a partner (if during 1999-2000) **4.3** / /
- Date you stopped being a partner (if during 1999-2000) **4.4** / /

Your share of the partnership's trading or professional income

Basis period begins **4.5** / / and ends **4.6** / /

- Your share of the profit or loss of this year's account for tax purposes **4.7** £
- Adjustment to arrive at profit or loss for this basis period **4.8** £
- Overlap profit brought forward **4.9** £ Deduct overlap relief used this year **4.10** £
- Overlap profit carried forward **4.11** £
- Adjustment for farmers' averaging (see Notes, page PN3 if the partnership made a loss in 1999-2000) or foreign tax deducted, if tax credit relief not claimed **4.12** £
- Adjustment on change of basis **4.12A** £

Net profit for 1999-2000 (if loss, enter '0' in box 4.13 and enter the loss in box 4.14) **4.13** £

Allowable loss for 1999-2000 **4.14** £

- Loss offset against other income for 1999-2000 **4.15** £
- Loss to carry back **4.16** £
- Loss to carry forward (that is, allowable loss not claimed in any other way) **4.17** £
- Losses brought forward from last year **4.18** £
- Losses brought forward from last year used this year **4.19** £

box 4.13 *minus* box 4.19
Taxable profit after losses brought forward **4.20** £

- Add amounts **not** included in the partnership accounts that are needed to calculate your taxable profit (for example, Enterprise Allowance (Business Start-up Allowance) received in 1999-2000) **4.21** £

box 4.20 + box 4.21
Total taxable profits from this business **4.22** £

Refer to Chapter 15 for the national insurance implications.

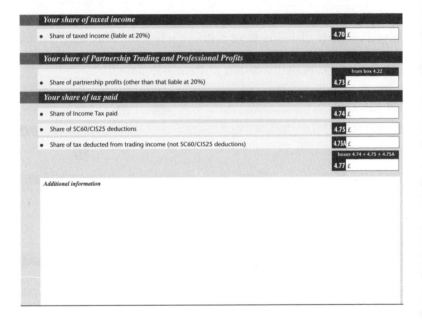

The supplementary pages headed **LAND AND PROPERTY** cover all types of rental income, whether it is from numerous properties, or a single rental, holiday lettings or qualifies for a Rent-a-Room relief. (Any income from land or property overseas should not be included here – ask for supplementary pages *Foreign*.)

The supplementary pages **Land and Property** are reproduced opposite.

To fill in these sections of the tax return you will need:

Records of rent received	
Records of expenses, and bills for them	

Pages 62–63 give you background details to the taxation of land and buildings, joint holdings and expenses payments that you might be able to claim.

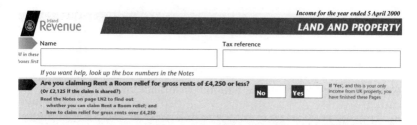

If you are only claiming Rent-a-Room relief you only need to tick the 'Yes' box. There is no need to fill in any other section. Refer to page 63 of this book for details of Rent-a-Room relief.

Is your income from furnished holiday lettings?
If 'No', turn over and fill in Page L2 to give details of your property income   No   Yes   If 'Yes', fill in boxes 5.1 to 5.18 before completing Page L2

Furnished holiday lettings

- Income from furnished holiday lettings — **5.1** £

■ *Expenses* (furnished holiday lettings only)

- Rent, rates, insurance, ground rents etc. — **5.2** £
- Repairs, maintenance and renewals — **5.3** £
- Finance charges, including interest — **5.4** £
- Legal and professional costs — **5.5** £
- Costs of services provided, including wages — **5.6** £
- Other expenses — **5.7** £

total of boxes 5.2 to 5.7 — **5.8** £

Net profit (put figures in brackets if a loss) — box 5.1 minus box 5.8 **5.9** £

■ *Tax adjustments*

- Private use — **5.10** £
- Balancing charges — **5.11** £ — box 5.10 + box 5.11 **5.12** £
- Capital allowances — **5.13** £

Profit for the year (copy to box 5.19). If loss, enter '0' in box 5.14 and put the loss in box 5.15 — boxes 5.9 + 5.12 minus box 5.13 **5.14** £

Loss for the year (if you have entered '0' in box 5.14) — boxes 5.9 + 5.12 minus box 5.13 **5.15** £

■ *Losses*

- Loss offset against 1999-2000 total income — **5.16** £
- Loss carried back — see Notes, page LN4 **5.17** £
- Loss offset against other income from property (copy to box 5.38) — see Notes, page LN4 **5.18** £

Other property income

■ Income

		copy from box 5.14		
• Furnished holiday lettings profits	**5.19** £			
• Rents and other income from land and property	**5.20** £		Tax deducted	
			5.21 £	
• Chargeable premiums	**5.22** £			boxes 5.19 + 5.20 + 5.22 + 5.22A
• Reverse premiums	**5.22A** £			**5.23** £

■ Expenses (do not include figures you have already put in boxes 5.2 to 5.7 on Page L1)

• Rent, rates, insurance, ground rents etc.	**5.24** £	
• Repairs, maintenance and renewals	**5.25** £	
• Finance charges, including interest	**5.26** £	
• Legal and professional costs	**5.27** £	
• Costs of services provided, including wages	**5.28** £	total of boxes 5.24 to 5.29
• Other expenses	**5.29** £	**5.30** £

Net profit (put figures in brackets if a loss) — box 5.23 *minus* box 5.30 — **5.31** £

■ Tax adjustments

• Private use	**5.32** £	box 5.32 + box 5.33
• Balancing charges	**5.33** £	**5.34** £
• Rent a Room exempt amount	**5.35** £	
• Capital allowances	**5.36** £	
• 10% wear and tear	**5.37** £	total of boxes 5.35 to 5.38
• Furnished holiday lettings losses (from box 5.18)	**5.38** £	**5.39** £

Adjusted profit (if loss enter '0' in box 5.40 and put the loss in box 5.41) — boxes 5.31 + 5.34 *minus* box 5.39 — **5.40** £

Adjusted loss (if you have entered '0' in box 5.40) — boxes 5.31 + 5.34 *minus* box 5.39 — **5.41** £

• Loss brought forward from previous year — **5.42** £

Profit for the year — box 5.40 *minus* box 5.42 — **5.43** £

■ Losses

• Loss offset against total income (read the note on page LN8)	**5.44** £
• Loss to carry forward to following year	**5.45** £
• Pooled expenses from 'one-estate election' carried forward	**5.46** £

Tick box 5.47 if these Pages include details of property let jointly — **5.47**

Now fill in any other supplementary Pages that apply to you.
Otherwise, go back to page 2 of your Tax Return and finish filling it in.

The supplementary pages headed **FOREIGN** cover all income, pensions and benefits that you receive from abroad.

These pages just apply to *income* from abroad. If you have made capital gains or losses, then these should be declared on the *capital gains* supplementary pages, although any foreign tax incurred should be stated here.

To fill in the **Foreign** pages you may need:

Overseas dividend vouchers	
Bank statements	
Details of overseas pensions and social security benefits	
Any foreign tax assessments	
Actual receipts for any foreign tax paid	

Note: Not all sections of the form are reproduced here.

Income and gains and tax credit relief for the year ended 5 April 2000

Revenue (Inland Revenue)

FOREIGN

Name _____ Tax reference _____

'l in these
oxes first

If you want help, look up the box numbers in the Notes

Foreign savings

Fill in columns A to E, and tick the box in column E if you want to claim tax credit relief.

	Country A (tick box if income is unremittable ▼)	Amount before tax B	UK tax C	Foreign tax D	Amount chargeable E (tick box to claim tax credit relief ▼)
Interest, and other income from overseas savings -see Notes, page FN4		£	£	£	£
		£	£	£	£
		£	£	£	£
			total of column above **6.1** £		total of column above **6.2** £
Dividends -see Notes, page FN4		£	£	£	£
		£	£	£	£
		£	£	£	£
			total of column above **6.1A** £		total of column above **6.2A** £

Foreign savings income taxable on the remittance basis and foreign income from overseas pensions or social security benefits, from land and property abroad, or income/benefits received from overseas trusts, companies and other entities

Fill in columns A to E, and tick the box in column E to claim tax credit relief.

	Country A (tick box if income is unremittable ▼)	Amount before tax B	UK tax C	Foreign tax D	Amount chargeable E (tick box to claim tax credit relief ▼)
Dividends, interest and other savings income taxable on the remittance basis -see Notes, page FN2		£	£	£	£
		£	£	£	£
		£	£	£	£
		£	£	£	£
		£	£	£	£
Pensions -see Notes, page FN5		£	£	£	£

■ *Social security benefits* - see Notes, page FN6		£	£	£	£	
		£	£	£	£	
		£	£	£	£	
		£	£	£	£	

■ *Income from land and property* **IMPORTANT** - see Notes, page FN6		£	£	£	£	

■ *Income received by an overseas trust, company, and other entity (excluding dividends)* - see Notes, page FN10		£	£	£	£	
		£	£	£	£	
		£	£	£	£	
		£	£	£	£	

total of column above **6.3** £   total of column above **6.4** £

■ *Dividend income received by an overseas trust, company or other entity* - see Notes, page FN10		£	£	£	£	
		£	£	£	£	
		£	£	£	£	
		£	£	£	£	

total of column above **6.3A** £   total of column above **6.4A** £

- Disposals of holdings in offshore funds, income from non-resident trusts and benefits received from overseas trusts, companies and other entities - *see Notes, page FN10.*   **6.5** £

Tick box 6.5A if you are omitting income from boxes 6.4, 6.4A or 6.5 - *see Notes, page FN11.*   **6.5A**

- Gains on foreign life insurance policies etc.   Number of years **6.6**   Tax treated as paid **6.7** £   Gains(s) **6.8** £

Tax credit relief for foreign tax paid on employment, self-employment and other income

See Notes, page FN13

Enter in this column the Page number in your Tax Return from which information is taken. Do this for each item for which you are claiming tax credit relief ▼	Country A	Foreign tax D	Amount chargeable E tick box to claim tax credit relief ▼	
		£	£	
		£	£	

- If you are calculating your tax, enter the total tax credit relief on your income in box 6.9   **6.9** £

Tax credit relief for foreign tax paid on chargeable gains reported on your Capital Gains Pages

See Notes, page FN14

Amount of gain under UK rules	Period over which UK gain accrued	Amount of gain under foreign tax rules	Period over which foreign gain accrued	Foreign tax paid D tick box to claim tax credit relief ▼
£	days £		days £	

- If you are calculating your tax, enter the total tax credit relief on your gains in box 6.10   **6.10** £

Income from land and property abroad

Address of property

Postcode

Having dealt with savings and other income the form then deals with income from land and property abroad and boxes 6.11 to 6.38 cover income, expenditure, losses and taxable profits.

The supplementary pages headed **TRUSTS ETC** enable you to declare any income you receive from trusts, settlements or estates of deceased persons. Tax deducted from such income may be at a different tax rate, and you need to identify these in the boxes.

To fill in these sections you will need:

Dividend and interest statements received from the Trustees or personal representatives	
Relevant correspondence identifying the type of trust, etc.	

See also page 64 for further details.

Inland Revenue — **Revenue**

Income for the year ended 5 April 2000

TRUSTS ETC

Name

Tax reference

I in these oxes first

If you want help, look up the box numbers in the Notes

Income from trusts and settlements

■ *Income taxed at:*

	Income receivable	Tax paid	Taxable amount
• 'rate applicable to trusts'	7.1 £	7.2 £	7.3 £
• basic rate	7.1A £	7.2A £	7.3A £
• the savings rate	7.4 £	7.5 £	7.6 £
• the dividend rate	7.4A £	7.5A £	7.6A £

Income from the estates of deceased persons

■ *Income bearing:*

	Income receivable	Tax paid	Taxable amount
• basic rate tax	7.7 £	7.8 £	7.9 £
• savings rate tax	7.10 £	7.11 £	7.12 £
• repayable dividend rate	7.13 £	7.14 £	7.15 £
• non-repayable basic rate tax	7.16 £	7.17 £	7.18 £
• non-repayable savings rate tax	7.19 £	7.20 £	7.21 £
• non-repayable dividend rate	7.22 £	7.23 £	7.24 £
• total foreign tax for which tax credit relief not claimed		7.25 £	

Additional information

The supplementary pages headed **CAPITAL GAINS** cover all capital gains and losses whether from stocks and shares, land and buildings, or other assets in the UK and overseas.

You have to fill in these sheets if you sold or gave away assets of £14,200 or more and your chargeable gains for tax purposes wre £7,100 or more in the year ended 5 April 2000.

To complete this section of the return you will need:

Copies of contract notes for the sale or purchase of shares	
Invoices and letters about the purchase and sale of other assets	
Invoices for allowable expenses which you can claim	

Chapter 16 of this book covers all aspects of capital gains.

Not all sections of the sheets are reproduced here. The first three pages of the capital gains sheets enable you to detail the relevant assets and then total them in boxes 8.1 to 8.6.

They are then summarised in boxes Q, U, L and O and 8.7 to 8.21 so as to record any gain or loss and any carried forward figures.

---

for the year ended 5 April 2000

Inland Revenue

CAPITAL GAINS

Chargeable gains and allowable losses

Once you have completed Page CG1, or Pages CG2 to CG6, fill in this Page.

Have you 'ticked' any row in Column B, 'Tick box if estimate or valuation used' on Pages CG1 or CG2?   **NO**   **YES**

Have you given details in Column G on Pages CG2 and CG3 of any Capital Gains reliefs claimed or due?   **NO**   **YES**

Enter the number of transactions from Page CG1 or column AA on Page CG2 for:

- transactions in quoted shares or securities   **box Q**
- transactions in unquoted shares or securities   **box U**
- transactions in land and property   **box L**
- other transactions   **box O**

Total taxable gains (from Page CG1 **or** Page CG3)   **8.7** £

Your taxable gains *minus* the annual exempt amount   box 8.7 minus £7,100   **8.8** £

Additional liability in respect of non-resident or dual resident trusts (see Notes, page CGN6)   **8.9** £

Capital losses

(Remember if your loss arose on a transaction with a connected person, see Notes page CGN13, you can only set that loss against gains you make on disposals to that same connected person.)

■ *This year's losses*

- Total (from box 8.2 on Page CG3 or box F2 on Page CG1)   **8.10** £
- Used against gains (total of column K1 on Page CG3, or the smaller of boxes F1 and F2 on Page CG1)   **8.11** £
- Used against earlier years' gains (generally only available to personal representatives, see Notes, page CGN11)   **8.12** £

Used against income (only losses of the type described on page CGN9 can be used against income)	8.13A £	amount claimed against income of 1999-2000	box 8.13A + box 8.13B	
	8.13B £	amount claimed against income of 1998-99	8.13 £	
This year's unused losses			box 8.10 *minus* (boxes 8.11+ 8.12+ 8.13) 8.14 £	

■ *Earlier years' losses*

Unused losses of 1996-97 and later years	8.15 £
Used this year (losses from box 8.15 are used in priority to losses from box 8.18) (column K3 on Page CG3 or box F6 on Page CG1)	8.16 £
Remaining unused losses of 1996-97 and later years	box 8.15 *minus* box 8.16 8.17 £
Unused losses of 1995-96 and earlier years	8.18 £
Used this year (losses from box 8.15 are used in priority to losses from box 8.18) (column K3 on Page CG3 or box F6 on Page CG1)	box 8.6 *minus* box 8.16 (or box F6 *minus* box 8.16) 8.19 £

■ *Total of unused losses to carry forward*

Carried forward losses of 1996-97 and later years	box 8.14 + box 8.17 8.20 £
Carried forward losses of 1995-96 and earlier years	box 8.18 *minus* box 8.19 8.21 £

The supplementary pages **NON-RESIDENCE ETC.** contain a sequence of questions to enable the tax office to determine whether you are:

not resident in the UK
not ordinarily resident in the UK
entitled to apportion income in the tax year
not domiciled in the UK

The rules governing the legal status of a person and the consequent tax implications are among some of the most difficult tax legislation and are outside the scope of this basic tax guide.

However, if you have requested these supplementary pages the tax office will automatically send you a set of extensive notes to help you decide your tax status.

Note: Not all sections of the forms are reproduced here.

Inland Revenue — *For the year ended 5 April 2000* — **NON-RESIDENCE ETC.**

Residence status

I am (please tick appropriate box)

resident in the UK	9.1	not resident in the UK	9.2
ordinarily resident in the UK	9.3	not ordinarily resident in the UK	9.4
not domiciled in the UK (and it is relevant to my Income Tax or Capital Gains Tax liability)	9.5	claiming split-year treatment	9.6
claiming personal allowances as a non-resident	9.7	resident in a country other than the UK (under a double taxation agreement) at the same time as being resident in the UK	9.8

Information required if you claim to be non-resident in the UK for the whole of 1999-2000

- Are you in any of the following categories:
  - a Commonwealth citizen (this includes a British citizen) or an EEA (European Economic Area) national?
  - a present or former employee of the British Crown (including a civil servant, member of the armed forces etc)?
  - a UK missionary society employee?
  - a civil servant in a territory under the protection of the British Crown?
  - a resident of the Isle of Man or the Channel Islands?
  - a former resident of the UK and you live abroad for the sake of your own health or the health of a member of your family who lives with you?
  - a widow or widower of an employee of the British Crown?

  Yes 9.9   No 9.10

- How many days have you spent in the UK, excluding days of arrival and departure, during the year ended 5 April 2000? *Enter the number of days*   9.11   days

- Were you resident in the UK for 1998-99?   Yes 9.12   No 9.13

- How many days have you spent in the UK up to 5 April 2000, excluding days of arrival and departure, since 5 April 1996 or, if later, the date you originally left the UK ? *Enter the number of days* 9.14   days

- What is your country of nationality?   9.15

- In which country are you resident?   9.16

Information required if you claim to be not ordinarily resident in the UK for the whole of 1999-2000

- Were you ordinarily resident in the UK for 1998-99?   Yes 9.17   No 9.18

- When you came to the UK, did you intend to stay here for at least three years?   Yes 9.19   No 9.20   Not applicable 9.21

- If you have left the UK, do you intend to live outside the UK permanently?   Yes 9.22   No 9.23   Not applicable 9.24

Information required if you claim split-year treatment

- Date of your arrival in the UK   9.25 Day / Month / Year

- Date of your departure from the UK   9.26 Day / Month / Year

Information required if you claim to be not domiciled in the UK

- Have you submitted full facts to the Inland Revenue (for example, on forms DOM1 or P86) regarding your domicile in the six years ended 5 April 2000?   Yes 9.27   No 9.28

- If you came to the UK before 6 April 1999, has there been a relevant change in your circumstances or intentions during the year ended 5 April 2000?   Yes 9.29   No 9.30   Not applicable 9.31

Information required if you are resident in the UK and you also claim to be resident in another country for the purposes of a Double Taxation Agreement

- In which country as well as the UK were you regarded as resident for 1999-2000?   9.32

- Were you also regarded as resident in the country in box 9.32 for 1998-99?   Yes 9.33   No 9.34

Information required if you are not resident or are resident in another country for the purpose of a Double Taxation Agreement and are claiming relief under a Double Taxation Agreement

- Amount of any relief you are claiming from UK tax if you are not resident in the UK or are dual resident   9.35 £

You must fill in and send me the claim form in *Help Sheet IR302: Dual residents* or *Help Sheet IR304: Non residents - relief under Double Taxation Agreements* as applicable. These are available from the Orderline.

Additional information

Having completed any supplementary pages that are relevant to you, you can now fill in pages 3 and 4 of the *main tax return*.

This section covers **INCOME** from investments, pensions, social security benefits and any other income not covered under other sections of the return.

The first two sections (Q10) cover Income from Savings and Investments. To fill in these you will need:

Interest statements and any tax deduction certificates from UK banks, building societies and deposit takers	
Details of any National Savings investments	
Dividend vouchers showing tax credits	

Although the tax office does not want you to list all your individual dividends and interest etc. in the tax form – you only have to put in the totals – you will need to keep the details in case you are asked for them. Use the blank working sheets on pages 136–137 of this book. See also page 64 for further advice.

INCOME *for the year ended 5 April 2000*

Q10 Did you receive any income from UK savings and investments? **NO** [ ] **YES** [ ] If yes, fill in boxes 10.1 to 10.26 as appropriate. Include only your share from any joint savings and investments.

■ *Interest*

● Interest from UK banks, building societies and deposit takers

- where **no tax** has been deducted — Taxable amount — **10.1** £

	Amount **after** tax deducted	Tax deducted	Gross amount **before** tax
- where **tax has** been deducted	**10.2** £	**10.3** £	**10.4** £
● Interest distributions from UK authorised unit trusts and open-ended investment companies (dividend distributions go below)	**10.5** £ (Amount after tax deducted)	**10.6** £ (Tax deducted)	**10.7** £ (Gross amount before tax)

● National Savings (other than FIRST Option Bonds and the first £70 of interest from a National Savings Ordinary Account) — Taxable amount — **10.8** £

	Amount after tax deducted	Tax deducted	Gross amount before tax
● National Savings FIRST Option Bonds	**10.9** £	**10.10** £	**10.11** £
● Other income from UK savings and investments (except dividends)	**10.12** £	**10.13** £	**10.14** £

■ *Dividends*

	Dividend/distribution	Tax credit	Dividend/distribution plus credit
● Dividends and other qualifying distributions from UK companies	**10.15** £	**10.16** £	**10.17** £

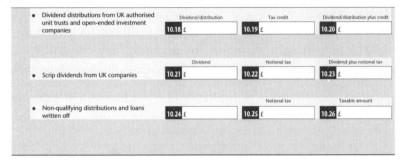

The next section (Q11) deals with U.K. pensions and social security benefits received.

To fill in this section you will need:

Your State pension book or details	
A P60 form or certificate of tax deducted in the case of any other pension	
DSS statements in respect of unemployment benefit, income support or jobseeker's allowance	
Details of any incapacity benefit or other taxable State benefit	

Do not include the State Christmas bonus or maternity allowance as they are not taxable. See page 58 for further details.

INCOME for the year ended 5 April 2000, continued

Q11 Did you receive a taxable UK pension, retirement annuity or Social Security benefit?
Read the notes on pages 12 to 14 of the Tax Return Guide.

NO ☐ YES ☐ If yes, fill in boxes 11.1 to 11.13 as appropriate.

■ *State pensions and benefits*

Taxable amount for 1999-2000

- State Retirement Pension (enter the total of your weekly entitlements for the year) — **11.1** £
- Widow's Pension — **11.2** £
- Widowed Mother's Allowance — **11.3** £
- Industrial Death Benefit Pension — **11.4** £
- Jobseeker's Allowance — **11.5** £
- Invalid Care Allowance — **11.6** £
- Statutory Sick Pay and Statutory Maternity Pay paid by the Department of Social Security — **11.7** £

	Tax deducted	Gross amount before tax
● Taxable Incapacity Benefit	**11.8** £	**11.9** £

■ *Other pensions and retirement annuities*

	Amount after tax deducted	Tax deducted	Gross amount before tax
● Pensions (other than State pensions) and retirement annuities	**11.10** £	**11.11** £	**11.12** £

	Amount of deduction	
● Deduction - see the note for box 11.13 on page 14 of your Tax Return Guide	**11.13** £	

Sections Q12 and Q13 deal with any other income that you may have received. Refer to the index at the back of this book for help.

Q13 in particular is useful for declaring any miscellaneous income from casual work, insurance or mail order commission, royalties, consultancy work etc., but make sure you claim any allowable expenses (see page 59) and only put the net figure in your tax return.

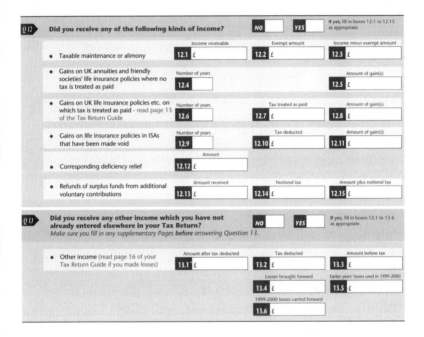

Use the blank working sheets on pages 136–137 if there is more than one figure to go in each box.

Having dealt with the income from all sources, the tax return now covers **RELIEFS AND ALLOWANCES** that you can claim as a deduction from your income.

First, the **Reliefs**. Q14 concentrates on relief for pension contributions. Refer to pages 97 and 130.

To fill in Q14 you will need pension statements that you would have received from the insurance company, or your employer.

If you do not want to claim relief on pension contributions just tick the 'No' box.

RELIEFS *for the year ended 5 April 2000*

Q14 **Do you want to claim relief for pension contributions?** [NO] [YES] If yes, fill in boxes 14.1 to 14.17 as appropriate.
Do not include contributions deducted from your pay by your employer to their pension scheme, because tax relief is given automatically. But **do include** your contributions to personal pension schemes and free-standing AVC schemes.

■ *Retirement annuity contracts*

Qualifying payments made in 1999-2000 **14.1** £	1999-2000 payments used in an earlier year **14.2** £	**Relief claimed**
1999-2000 payments now to be carried back **14.3** £	Payments brought back from 2000-2001 **14.4** £	box 14.1 *minus* (boxes 14.2 and 14.3, but not 14.4) **14.5** £

■ *Self-employed contributions to personal pension plans*

Qualifying payments made in 1999-2000 **14.6** £	1999-2000 payments used in an earlier year **14.7** £	**Relief claimed**
1999-2000 payments now to be carried back **14.8** £	Payments brought back from 2000-2001 **14.9** £	box 14.6 *minus* (boxes 14.7 and 14.8, but not 14.9) **14.10** £

■ *Employee contributions to personal pension plans* **(include your gross contribution** - see the note on box 14.11 in your Tax Return Guide)

Qualifying payments made in 1999-2000 **14.11** £	1999-2000 payments used in an earlier year **14.12** £	**Relief claimed**
1999-2000 payments now to be carried back **14.13** £	Payments brought back from 2000-2001 **14.14** £	box 14.11 *minus* (boxes 14.12 and 14.13, but not 14.14) **14.15** £

■ *Contributions to other pension schemes and free-standing AVC schemes*

● Amount of contributions to employer's schemes **not deducted** at source from pay **14.16** £

● Gross amount of free-standing additional voluntary contributions paid in 1999-2000 **14.17** £

Boxes **14.1** to **14.17** see pages 130 and 131.

The next section, Q15 covers all other **Reliefs**. In the main you will need statements or certificates from third parties from which to get the information.

If you do not want to claim any of these reliefs, just tick the 'No' box.

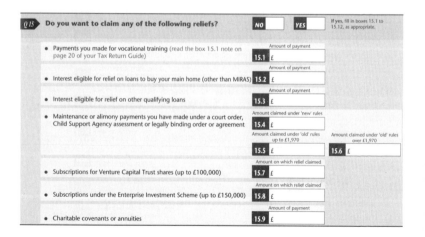

Q15 **Do you want to claim any of the following reliefs?** [NO] [YES] If yes, fill in boxes 15.1 to 15.12, as appropriate.

● Payments you made for vocational training (read the box 15.1 note on page 20 of your Tax Return Guide) — Amount of payment **15.1** £

● Interest eligible for relief on loans to buy your main home (other than MIRAS) — Amount of payment **15.2** £

● Interest eligible for relief on other qualifying loans — Amount of payment **15.3** £

● Maintenance or alimony payments you have made under a court order, Child Support Agency assessment or legally binding order or agreement — Amount claimed under 'new' rules **15.4** £ / Amount claimed under 'old' rules up to £1,970 **15.5** £ / Amount claimed under 'old' rules over £1,970 **15.6** £

● Subscriptions for Venture Capital Trust shares (up to £100,000) — Amount on which relief claimed **15.7** £

● Subscriptions under the Enterprise Investment Scheme (up to £150,000) — Amount on which relief claimed **15.8** £

● Charitable covenants or annuities — Amount of payment **15.9** £

	Amount of qualifying payments
● Gift Aid and Millennium Gift Aid	**15.10** £

	Amount of payment
● Post-cessation expenses, pre-incorporation losses brought forward and losses on relevant discounted securities, etc.	**15.11** £

	Half amount of payment
● Payments to a trade union or friendly society for death benefits	**15.12** £

Box no. **15.1**   see page 66   Box no. **15.7**   see page 128

Box no. **15.2**   see page 66   Box no. **15.8**   see page 128

Box no. **15.3**   see page 68   Box no. **15.9**   see page 71

Box no. **15.4**   see page 70   Box no. **15.10**   see page 71

Box no. **15.5**   see page 70   Box no. **15.11**   see page 109

Box no. **15.6**   see page 70   Box no. **15.12**   see page 71

The **ALLOWANCES** section of the return (Q16) is your chance to claim the married couple's allowance, the additional personal allowance, the transitional allowance and the blind person's and widow's bereavement allowance.

Chapter 9 gives background details to all these allowances including the option you have to transfer surplus allowances to your wife or husband.

ALLOWANCES for the year ended 5 April 2000

Q 16 You get your personal allowance of £4,335 automatically. **If you were born before 6 April 1935, enter your date of birth in box 21.4** - you may get higher age-related allowances.

Do you want to claim any of the following allowances?   **NO**   **YES**   If yes, please read pages 23 to 26 of your Tax Return Guide and then fill in boxes 16.1 to 16.28 as appropriate.

■ *Blind person's allowance*   Date of registration (if first year of claim) **16.1** / /   Local authority (or other register) **16.2**

■ *Transitional allowance (for some wives with husbands on low income if received in earlier years).*

● Tick to claim and give details in the 'Additional information' box on page 8   **16.3**
   (please see page 23 of your Tax Return Guide for what is needed)

● If you want to calculate your tax, enter the amount of transitional allowance you can have in box 16.4   **16.4** £

■ *Married couple's allowance for a married man - see page 24 of your Tax Return Guide.*

● Wife's full name   **16.5**   ● Date of marriage (if after 5 April 1999)   **16.6** / /

● Wife's date of birth (if before 6 April 1935)   **16.7** / /   ● Tick box 16.8 if you or your wife have allocated **half** the allowance to her   **16.8**

box number 16.9 is not used   ● Tick box 16.10 if you and your wife have allocated **all** the allowance to her   **16.10**

■ *Married couple's allowance for a married woman - see page 24 of your Tax Return Guide.*

● Date of marriage (if after 5 April 1999)   **16.11** / /

● Husband's full name   **16.12**   ● Tick box 16.13 if you or your husband have allocated **half** the allowance to you   **16.13**

box number 16.14 is not used   ● Tick box 16.15 if you and your husband have allocated **all** the allowance to you   **16.15**

■ *Additional personal allowance (available in some circumstances if you have a child living with you - see page 25 of your Tax Return Guide).*

- Tick box 16.16A if you are claiming the married couple's allowance **and** additional personal allowance because your spouse was unable to look after themselves because of illness or disablement, throughout the year ended 5 April 2000   **16.16A**

- Name of the child claimed for   **16.16**

- Child's date of birth   **16.17**   /   /
- Tick if child lived with you for at least part of the year ended 5 April 2000   **16.18**

- Name of university etc/type of training if the child is 16 or over on 6 April 1999 and in full time education or training   **16.19**

Sharing a claim

Name and address of other person claiming

16.20

- Enter your share as a percentage   **16.21**   %
- If share not agreed, enter the number of days in the year ended 5 April 2000 that the child lived with

Postcode

- you   **16.22**   days
- other person   **16.23**   days

■ *Widow's bereavement allowance*   • Date of your husband's death   **16.24**   /   /

■ *Transfer of surplus allowances - see page 26 of your Tax Return Guide before you fill in boxes 16.25 to 16.28.*

- Tick if you want your spouse to have your unused allowances   **16.25**
- Tick if you want to have your spouse's unused allowances   **16.26**

Please give details in the 'Additional information' box on page 8 - *see page 26 of your Tax Return Guide for what is needed.*

If you want to calculate your tax, enter the amount of the surplus allowance you can have.

- Blind person's surplus allowance   **16.27** £
- Married couple's surplus allowance   **16.28** £

The final section of your tax return asks some general questions headed **OTHER INFORMATION** (Q17–Q23).

You must decide here whether you want to calculate your own tax liability (or refund). If you do NOT then tick the 'No' box and you need not fill in any further boxes under Q18.

If 'Yes', then turn to page 133 in this book where the tax calculation sheets are reproduced.

Under section Q19 (overleaf), if you think a repayment of tax is due to you then fill in the relevant personal information.

Q20 and Q21 also need completing with your personal details.

OTHER INFORMATION *for the year ended 5 April 2000*

Q17 Have you already had any 1999-2000 tax refunded or set off by your Inland Revenue office or the Benefits Agency (in Northern Ireland, the Social Security Agency)? *Read the notes on page 26 of your Tax Return Guide*   **NO**   **YES**
If yes, enter the amount of the refund in box 17.1.   **17.1** £

Q18 Do you want to calculate your tax?   **NO**   **YES**
If yes, do it now and then fill in boxes 18.1 to 18.9. Your Tax Calculation Guide will help.

- Unpaid tax for earlier years **included in your tax code for 1999-2000**   **18.1** £

- Tax due for 1999-2000 included in your tax code for a later year   **18.2** £

- Total tax and Class 4 NIC due for 1999-2000 **before** you made any payments on account *(put the amount in brackets if an overpayment)*   **18.3** £

- Tax due for earlier years   **18.4** £

- Tick box 18.5 if you have calculated tax overpaid for earlier years (and enter the amount in the 'Additional information' box on page 8)   **18.5**

- Your first payment on account for 2000-2001 *(include the pence)*   **18.6** £
Tick box 18.7 if you are making a claim to reduce your 2000-2001 payments on account and say why in the 'Additional information' box   **18.7**   Tick box 18.8 if you do **not** need to make 2000-2001 payments on account   **18.8**

- Tick box 18.9 if you are reclaiming 2000-2001 tax now (and enter the amount in the 'Additional information' box on page 8)   **18.9**

Q19 Do you want to claim a repayment if you have paid too much tax? *(If you tick 'No' or the tax you have overpaid is below £10, I will use the amount you are owed to reduce your next tax bill.)*

NO   YES   If yes, fill in boxes 19.1A to 19.12 as appropriate.

Should the repayment be sent:

• direct to your bank or building society account?
Tick box 19.1A and fill in boxes 19.3 to 19.7   **19.1A**

or

by cheque to you at your home address?
Tick box 19.1B   **19.1B**

OR

• to a nominee? Tick box 19.2 and fill in boxes 19.3 to 19.12 as appropriate   **19.2**

Fill in boxes 19.3 to 19.7 if the repayment is to be sent to your own, or your nominees' bank or building society account

Name of bank or building society   **19.3**

Branch sort code   **19.4**   –   –

Account number   **19.5**

Name of account   **19.6**

Building society ref.   **19.7**

• If your nominee is your agent, tick box 19.8   **19.8**

Agent's reference for you (if your agent is your nominee)   **19.9**

Name of your nominee/agent

I authorise   **19.10**

Nominee/agent address   **19.11**

Postcode

to receive on my behalf the amount due

This authority must be signed by you. A photocopy of your signature will not do.   **19.12**   Signature

Q20 Are your details on the front of the Tax Return wrong?   NO   YES   If yes, please make any corrections on the front of the form.

Q21 Please give other personal details in boxes 21.1 to 21.6. *This information helps us to be more efficient and effective and may support claims you have made elsewhere in your Tax Return.*

Please give a daytime telephone number if convenient. It is often simpler to phone if we need to ask you about your Tax Return.

Your telephone number   **21.1**

or, if you prefer, your agent's telephone number   **21.2**
(also give your agent's name and reference in the 'Additional information' box on page 8)

Enter your first two forenames   **21.5**

Say if you are single, married, widowed, divorced or separated   **21.3**

Date of birth   **21.4**   /   /
Enter your date of birth if you are self-employed, or you were born before 6 April 1935, or you have ticked the 'Yes' box in Question 14, or you are claiming relief for Venture Capital Trust subscriptions

Enter your National Insurance number (if known)   **21.6**

The final page of the tax return asks some general questions – Other Information – so that the tax office know how to handle your tax affairs or calculate your tax code for 2000–2001.

Box 22.2 in particular, gives you the option of not paying any tax liability due through your PAYE tax code – for example you may not want your employer to know that you have other income or have made other profits or gains.

Finally, tick the boxes under Q23 to indicate any supplementary pages you are attaching to your tax return. Then sign and date the declaration.

OTHER INFORMATION *for the year ended 5 April 2000, continued*

Q22 Please tick boxes 22.1 to 22.5 if they apply and provide any additional information in the box below.

Tick box 22.1 if you expect to receive a new pension or Social Security benefit in 2000-2001.   **22.1**

Tick box 22.2 if you do **not** want any tax you owe for 1999-2000 collected through your tax code.   **22.2**

Tick box 22.3 if this Tax Return contains figures that are provisional because you do not yet have final figures. Page 27 of your Tax Return Guide explains the circumstances in which Tax Returns containing provisional figures may be accepted and tells you what you must enter in the box below.   **22.3**

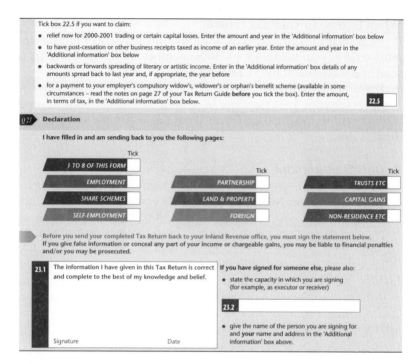

Tick box 22.5 if you want to claim:

- relief now for 2000-2001 trading or certain capital losses. Enter the amount and year in the 'Additional information' box below
- to have post-cessation or other business receipts taxed as income of an earlier year. Enter the amount and year in the 'Additional information' box below
- backwards or forwards spreading of literary or artistic income. Enter in the 'Additional information' box details of any amounts spread back to last year and, if appropriate, the year before
- for a payment to your employer's compulsory widow's, widower's or orphan's benefit scheme (available in some circumstances – read the notes on page 27 of your Tax Return Guide **before** you tick the box). Enter the amount, in terms of tax, in the 'Additional information' box below. **22.5**

Q23 Declaration

I have filled in and am sending back to you the following pages:

	Tick		Tick		Tick
1 TO 8 OF THIS FORM					
EMPLOYMENT		PARTNERSHIP		TRUSTS ETC	
SHARE SCHEMES		LAND & PROPERTY		CAPITAL GAINS	
SELF-EMPLOYMENT		FOREIGN		NON-RESIDENCE ETC	

Before you send your completed Tax Return back to your Inland Revenue office, you must sign the statement below. If you give false information or conceal any part of your income or chargeable gains, you may be liable to financial penalties and/or may be prosecuted.

23.1 The information I have given in this Tax Return is correct and complete to the best of my knowledge and belief.

If you have signed for someone else, please also:

- state the capacity in which you are signing (for example, as executor or receiver)

23.2

- give the name of the person you are signing for and **your** name and address in the 'Additional information' box above.

Signature   Date

When you sign your tax return you are declaring that to the best of your knowledge and belief, the return is complete, true and accurate.

It is often thought that if you keep quiet about some of your income, then the tax inspector will not find out about it. This is not the case. The tax authorities have many sources of information, the most common being your employer, banks, building societies and other businesses, all of whom may be required to make a return of payments made to individuals and businesses.

As the tax return and most of the supplementary pages have been reproduced in this book you could fill them in so you have a permanent record, remembering also to use the working sheets at the back of the book.

Do not worry if you have forgotten to claim an allowance due to you, for you have a time limit of six years in which to tell your tax office of your mistake. Therefore you can go back to 6 April 1993 to check your tax and possibly get a refund – and interest too.

If you forget to include some of your income on the form you should immediately notify your tax office explaining your error.

When to send in your tax return

If you want the tax office to calculate your tax liability or refund you must send in your tax return by 30 September 2000 – they will then send you a statement by 31 January 2001.

If you wish to use the tax calculator and calculate your own tax liability (see page 133) then you have until 31 January 2001 to send in your return, in which case you should also pay the tax that you think is due.

Payments on account

Some people with several sources of untaxed income, and the self-employed, will have to make two payments on account for each tax year, e.g. for the year ended 5 April 2000 the first payment of 50 per cent of your anticipated tax bill should have been made by 31 January 2000 and the second 50 per cent on 31 July 2000; any balance due, once your tax liability is agreed, being payable on 31 January 2001, although a refund may be dealt with as soon as agreed.

It is up to you to work out how much you need to pay on account. If you disagree with any figure that the tax office has demanded then ask for form SA303 on which you can explain your reasons.

Interest will be charged on any amount paid late.

Surcharges and penalties

There will be an automatic penalty of £100 if your tax return is not sent in by 31 January 2001 and another £100 six months later if it is still overdue. These are reduced if the tax due is less than £200. However, a tribunal may award a penalty of up to £60 a day and, if the return is 12 months late, there is a further penalty of up to 100 per cent of the tax liability.

In addition, a surcharge will be charged on any tax not paid on the due date – five per cent of any tax due by 31 January if unpaid at 28 February, and a further five per cent if unpaid by 31 July (plus interest on the first surcharge).

There are also fines of up to £3,000 for each failure to keep adequate records to support figures in your tax return.

Problems with your tax office

Contact your tax enquiry office initially if you have a query; then your tax inspector. If you still do not get satisfaction write to the District Inspector or Inland Revenue adjudicator or as a last resort the Regional Controller – all telephone numbers are in the telephone directory under Inland Revenue.

CHAPTER FIVE

Your 2000 Tax Return
Pay, perks and pensions

This chapter deals with income from employment including any benefits or expense allowances, and redundancy or leaving compensation you have received. Any pensions and social security benefits are also covered here.

Wages, salaries, fees, bonuses, etc.

You should have received from your employer a Form P60 which shows your earnings for the year and tax deducted under PAYE. You are entitled by law to receive this form by 31 May so chase your employer if it is not to hand.

Also include in the *Employment* section of the tax return any wages you received from your husband or wife if you were employed in his or her business.

You must show your gross earnings before any deductions of income tax, national insurance, etc. but you are allowed to deduct any contributions you make to your employer's pension scheme provided that it is one approved by the tax inspector.

Your P60 form may include pay from a previous employer in which case it needs to be shown on a separate *Employment* page, as you need one for each employer; or it may include payments for unemployment benefits, income support or Jobseeker's allowance: these must be shown separately on page 4, the *Income* section of your tax return.

Directors' remuneration is frequently voted on an annual basis. The amount to show in your tax return is usually the amount actually received in the tax year (normally the figure on your P60 form); however, you are taxable on earnings shown in the company's accounts if such sums were *available* (even if not actually drawn by you) in the tax year.

In addition to your regular PAYE employment, you may have other earnings. These might include casual work, fees and commissions, etc. Do not enter such income in this section, but under the *Income* section of your tax return (Q13) – see page 41 in this book.

Make sure you claim any relevant expenses (see page 59).

Tips and gratuities, if not included in your P60 form, should, however, be shown in box 1.9.

Under self assessment, if you are employed, then you must keep all records of earnings, income, benefits and expenses, etc. for 22 months after the end of the tax year.

Profit-related pay (PRP)

These schemes are being phased out and no relief is available for profit periods beginning on or after 1 January 2000. There has been a gradual reduction in the tax-free limits: for profit periods that began between 1 January 1998 and 31 December 1998 the limit was £2,000, or 20 per cent of total pay if lower, and for profit periods beginning between 1 January 1999 and 31 December 1999 the limit was £1,000, or 20 per cent of total pay if lower.

Details of profit-related pay relief does not have to be identified separately in your tax return as your employer will have deducted it to calculate your gross earnings on your P60 form (see page 48).

Leaving payments and compensation

Compensation for loss of office, payment in lieu of notice, ex-gratia payments, redundancy pay and retirement and death lump sums all come under this heading in the tax return.

The first £30,000 of compensation is tax free, but any excess is taxable.

Note, however, that if your contract of employment gives you a right to compensation on ceasing to be employed, then the lump sum you receive will be taxable, regardless of the amount.

When considering agreements for compensation, it is wise to consult a tax adviser or solicitor to negotiate the terms and the timing, which can be critical, especially on termination of a contract.

Any benefits arising after termination will be taxed only when they are actually received or 'enjoyed', rather than being taken into account in the actual redundancy year.

On the following page is an example of the various tax calculations that have to be considered when assessing the impact of redundancy pay.

Here is an example of the tax calculations arising on the receipt of redundancy pay:

John was made redundant during the 1999–2000 tax year.

His total earnings for the year were £33,100 and he was awarded a redundancy payment of £90,000.

			£
Earnings			33,100
less: Personal allowance, say			4,335
			£28,765
Tax liability	£ 1,500 at 10%		150
	£26,500 at 23%		6,095
	£ 765 at 40%		306
	£28,765	Tax due	£6,551

A redundancy payment of £90,000 is to be made after the form P45 has been issued. The *employer* will deduct tax as follows:

	£
Redundancy	90,000
Less: Tax-free limit	30,000
	60,000
Less: Tax on £60,000 at 23%	13,800
	£46,200

Once the employer has notified the tax office of this redundancy payment then they will review the tax position as follows:

		£
Earnings		33,100
Add: Redundancy after tax-free limit		60,000
		93,100
Less: Personal allowance		4,335
		£88,765
Tax liability calculated as:		£
£ 1,500 at 10%		150
£26,500 at 23%		6,095
£60,765 at 40%		24,306
£88,765		£30,551
Less: Tax already collected		
(as above)	£ 6,551	
Deducted from redundancy payment	13,800	20,351
Additional tax due		£10,200

When John sends in his 2000 self assessment tax return he will include the redundancy payment and will be sent either a tax demand, or, if he elects to calculate his own tax, will pay any tax due to the tax office by 31 January 2001.

Expense allowances

Round sum allowances are taxable as income unless an employee (and such term includes a director) can identify accurately the expenditure involved and satisfy the tax office that such sums were spent wholly, exclusively and necessarily on the employer's business.

Refer also to Chapter Six – 'Claiming expenses against your income'.

Benefits

Company cars

Virtually all employees whose earnings, reimbursed expenses *including* potential benefits in kind, are at the rate of £8,500 a year or more, and all directors whatever their earnings and expenses, are liable to pay tax on the 'benefit' they have from the use of a company car, and additionally on any fuel used on private journeys if paid for by their employer. These benefits will still be taxable if the car is used by a member of the employee's family or household. Company car and fuel benefits should appear in your coding notice, or tax assessment and need to be checked against the information provided by your employer.

The car benefit tax applies to all company cars, including those that are leased, and they will be assumed by your tax office to cover all the running costs, even if these amount to more than the tax benefit charge. The cost of a chauffeur, however, will be taxed as a separate benefit.

Company car benefit

The annual tax benefit for 1999–2000 is calculated as a percentage of the manufacturer's list price when new (less any personal contribution up to £5,000) – and includes delivery charges, VAT and any accessories over £100 added to the vehicle, unless they were for disabled persons.

The percentages are based on the list price and your annual business mileage as follows:

    List price × 35% business mileage under 2,500;
             × 25% business mileage 2,500 to 17,999;
             × 15% business mileage 18,000 and over.

This benefit is reduced by 25% for cars aged four years old or more at the end of the tax year.

In the case of second cars, the tax charge for 1999–2000 was 35 per cent below 18,000 business miles and 25 per cent for 18,000 miles or over.

Any contributions made towards the cost of the car by an employee (up to a maximum of £5,000) can be deducted from the list price figure before calculating the tax benefit.

It is irrelevant whether the car is second-hand or new – the list price at the time of first registration is the operative price subject to the above age and mileage reductions – unless it is a 'classic' car, aged 15 years or more at the end of the tax year with a market value of £15,000 or more, in which case the open market value is taken. A cap of £80,000 applies to both the list price and market value of classic cars.

Example of car benefit for 1999–2000

Car list price £12,500 when first registered in March 1994, annual business mileage 9,500.

Car benefit: 25% of £12,500	£3,125
less: 25% for age of the car	781
Taxable amount 1999–2000	£2,344

If the business mileage had been 18,500 miles, and the employee had contributed £1,000 towards the cost, then the taxable benefit would be:

Car benefit: 15% × (£12,500 – £1,000)	£1,725
less: 25% for age of the car	431
Taxable amount 1999–2000	£1,294

Benefit will not usually be taxable if the company cars are part of a 'pool' provided that the vehicle is actually used by two or more employees, with any private use being merely incidental, and the vehicle is not normally kept overnight at or near the employee's place of residence.

If a company car is not available for a period of at least 30 consecutive days (for example, it is in for repair) then the car benefit is reduced proportionately.

Company car private fuel benefit

If your employer pays for fuel used on private journeys (and this includes travel from home to your normal business address) then you are taxed on the benefits as follows regardless of your annual business mileage level:

| | 1999–2000 | | 2000–2001 | |
	Petrol	Diesel	Petrol	Diesel
	£	£	£	£
1,400cc or less	1,210	1,540	1,700	2,170
1,401cc to 2,000cc	1,540	1,540	2,170	2,170
Over 2000cc	2,270	2,270	3,200	3,200

Is there any way in which you can avoid the fuel tax charge?

Yes – you can pay for *all* your own private fuel (or reimburse your employer for *all* the private usage) but if you do this you will have to keep a detailed record each year of every car journey undertaken, both private and business. Bear in mind that travel from your home to your normal place of business is considered to be private mileage for tax purposes.

You may well find it to your advantage to accept the tax charge – it might be less than you would actually pay for private mileage!

The tax charge is the maximum that can be levied, even if in practice the cost of private mileage is more.

Company vans

Employees benefiting from the private use of a company van pay income tax on a standard 'benefit' of £500 a year (£350 for vans four or more years old). There is no fuel charge. The benefit is apportioned in the case of shared vans.

Mileage allowances

If an employee uses their own car for business journeys, either the employee can claim the *actual* costs, supported by detailed receipts, or claim a fixed mileage allowance using the Inland Revenue's authorised mileage rates.

There will be no taxable benefit if the mileage allowance claimed does not exceed the limits laid down by the tax office (see below). This applies whether the amount is reimbursed by the employer or the sum is not reimbursed but is claimed as a deduction in the employee's tax return.

Any payment in excess of these rates will be taxable. Many employers declare details of such profits to the tax office under the Fixed Profit Car Scheme, in which case you need not record details on your tax return.

Any mileage allowances paid to volunteer drivers in excess of the rates below will be taxable as a profit and should be declared on the individual's tax return.

The 'tax free' mileage rates for 2000–2001 are the same as for 1999–2000 and are assumed to include depreciation, servicing, repairs, insurance, road tax and all running costs (fuel, etc.):

	Cars up to 1,000cc	Cars 1,001 –1,500cc	Cars 1,501 –2,000cc	Cars over 2,000cc
On the first 4,000 miles in the tax year	28p	35p	45p	63p
On each mile over 4,000 miles in the tax year	17p	20p	25p	36p
The average of the two middle bands is 40p and 22.5p respectively and applies where your employer pays the rate irrespective of engine size.				

There are mileage allowances for bicycles of 12p a business mile and for motor cycles, as from 6 April 2000, of 24p.

Mobile telephones

All mobile telephones, including those fitted in cars, provided free of charge by employers, were assessable as a benefit in kind in the sum of £200 a year up to and including 1998–99 regardless of the type and value. As with car benefits, the benefit could be reduced if you were required to reimburse your employer with the whole cost of all private usage. **This tax charge was abolished from 6 April 1999.**

Living accommodation

Unless there are exceptional circumstances, living accommodation provided by an employer is taxable as a benefit.

The amount assessed will normally equate to the gross rateable value of the property, but if the cost of the property is higher than £75,000 then an *additional* amount is taxable, based on the market value of the property, less £75,000, multiplied by the official rate of interest (this interest rate is laid down by the Inland Revenue and fluctuates with market rates).

Any rent or contribution to upkeep you made to your employer is deductible from the benefit before calculating tax due.

Low-interest loan

An employee who has the benefit of a cheap or interest-free loan is taxable on the benefit as compared with the official rate of interest, but can claim tax relief at the appropriate rate if the loan is for an eligible purpose.

If the total of non-eligible loans does not exceed £5,000 at any time in the tax year, no charge is made.

Other benefits

All employees whose earnings, expenses and potential benefits are at the rate of £8,500 a year or more and most directors, regardless of their earnings or expenses, will probably have had any benefits or perks they have received reported to the tax inspector by their employer. (The employer has to do this by law by sending in a Form P11D, to which you are entitled to a copy from your employer by 6 July.) However, it is still your responsibility to declare such a 'perk' in your tax return. There are certain benefits or perks which an employer can provide which are tax free. You need not mention the 'perk' on your tax return if it is not taxable, but see page 61 for dispensations, etc.

Some of the more usual benefits, with a summary of the tax situation, are detailed below.

Benefit	Employees earning £8,500 a year or more and directors	Employees earning less than £8,500 a year
Assets provided for your use free of charge (e.g. video)	Taxable at 20% of initial market value	Usually tax free
Canteen facilities available to directors and staff	Not taxable	Not taxable

Benefit	Employees earning £8,500 a year or more and directors	Employees earning less than £8,500 a year
Cash vouchers	Taxable	Taxable
Child care facilities	Not taxable (but see page 77)	Not taxable
Clothing and other goods given to you by your employer	Taxable	Taxed on second-hand value
Company cars, vans, etc.	Taxable at varying rates	Not taxable
Computer equipment	Not taxable on first £2,500 of computer's value	
Credit cards (for personal, not business expenditure)	Taxable	Taxable
Exam prizes	Not taxable if reasonable and not part of employment contract	
Fuel for private use	Taxable at scale rate	Not taxable
Holidays	Taxable apart from business element	If employer pays directly, tax-free
Interest-free loan	Normally taxable	Not taxable
In-house benefits	Taxable only on the value of the marginal or additional cost to the employer	
Jobfinder's grant	Not taxable	Not taxable
Living accommodation	Normally taxable at annual value unless essential for your employment	
Luncheon vouchers	Tax free up to 15p per working day	
Mobile telephones	Not taxable	Not taxable
Outplacement counselling	Not taxable	Not taxable
Pension contributions and death in service cover	Normally tax-free	
Private health schemes	Taxable	Not taxable
Prizes and incentive awards	Taxable	Taxable
Relocation expenses	Tax-free up to £8,000	
Scholarships provided by employers' trust	Taxable	Not taxable
Season tickets for travel paid directly by employer	Taxable	Taxable
Share incentive schemes approved by tax inspector	Not taxable (but see below)	Not taxable

Benefit	Employees earning £8,500 a year or more and directors	Employees earning less than £8,500 a year
Sick pay schemes	Taxable	Taxable
Workplace sports facilities	Not taxable	Not taxable

Share schemes

Savings-related share schemes (save as you earn)

Employees pay a monthly sum via their employer into a savings-related share option scheme over a predetermined period at the end of which, the savings, plus a tax-free bonus, are used to purchase shares at a fixed price. This price must not be less than 80 per cent of the market value at the time of the option. No income tax or National Insurance should be payable on the option grant or on exercising the option.

No capital gain arose if shares up to the value of £3,000 were transferred into a single company PEP within certain time limits and this applies similarly to ISAs (up to the annual limit) from 6 April 1999.

Company share option schemes

An employer grants to an employee an option to purchase shares at a fixed price (which must not be discounted) at a future date. No income tax or National Insurance is payable on the granting of the option nor on any proceeds of sale, provided the option was taken out after 28 April 1996 and the total value of approved options did not exceed £30,000. There are additional rules for options taken out before this date and for options exercised more frequently than once every three years.

Approved profit sharing schemes

An employer allocates shares to employees and places them in a trust approved by the Inland Revenue. The maximum annual value for each employee is £3,000 or 10 per cent of their annual earnings (excluding benefits but after deducting pension contributions), whichever is the greater, subject to a ceiling of £8,000.

Provided you hold the shares for a minimum of two years no income tax or National Insurance is payable on the allocation of the shares; nor on any profit when you sell the shares if held for at least three years.

In all cases, capital gains tax may be payable on the proceeds of sale (see page 114). Employees may transfer the shares into an ISA free of capital gains tax, subject to certain restrictions.

Employment abroad (foreign earnings)

There are supplementary pages to the tax return which specifically deal with people who normally live in the UK but have income or earnings from overseas. (See page 32).

The general foreign earnings deduction available for earnings from an employment carried out abroad during a qualifying period of 365 days or more was abolished with effect from 17 March 1998 although it continues to apply to seafarers.

There are, however, measures which are intended to protect employees from double taxation in both the UK and the host country; principally the double taxation agreements held with various countries throughout the world.

If you receive a pension as a result of overseas employment, you will normally get a minimum of a 10 per cent deduction.

Before you take up an appointment abroad, be sure to check very carefully, both with your employer and with your tax office, as to how foreign earnings in your particular instance will be treated for tax purposes.

Income from pension and benefits

Under the *Income* section of the tax return (Q11) you have to state income you have received from the following pensions and social security allowances:

State retirement pension
Widow's pension and widowed mother's allowance
Industrial death benefit pension
Unemployment benefit and jobseeker's allowance
Invalid care allowance and any taxable incapacity benefit
Statutory sick pay and statutory maternity pay if it is not included in the P60 form given to you by your employer.

You also have to state other pension income you have received, including retirement annuities, and make a note of any tax deducted. If you have such pensions, it is important that you check how much tax you have paid at the end of each tax year (5 April) to see if you are due a refund. (See page 92.)

CHAPTER SIX

Your 2000 Tax Return Claiming expenses against your income

There are certain types of expenditure which, if *necessary* for your job and provided at your expense, may be claimed against your income. Fill in the appropriate boxes in the 'expenses' section of the *Employment* page of your tax return. A good test of whether a claim will succeed is to obtain from your employer a letter confirming that while your expenses arejustified and necessary for your job, they are not reimbursed as a matter of policy.

It is important to keep a record of the details and dates on which the expenditure was incurred, and the bills where possible. Some allowable expenses are listed below.

Factory, manual and shop workers

Extra costs incurred by employees working temporarily away from home, for example a lunch allowance of £2 per day if travelling away from the factory or office. Lorry drivers and construction site workers have special concessions.

Overalls, boiler suits, boots, helmets, gloves and other special protective clothing. You should also include the cost of cleaning and repairing such items.

Tools, toolbags and equipment.

Travelling expenses (but see page 60).

Trade journals and technical books essential to your job.

Trade unions often agree with the tax inspector a fixed allowance which you can claim to cover certain expenses (e.g. engineers £45 to £120; agricultural workers £70). Alternatively, keep a record of all your expenses and submit an annual claim.

Healthcare workers

A set of flat rate expenses were introduced in 1998–99 and your tax office will consider claims for the six years prior to the current tax year.

Salesmen, office and clerical workers

Travelling and hotel expenses on company business.

Car expenses, with the exception of those relating to your private journeys. These should be claimed only after the deduction of any contributions made by your employer.

If you use your own car for business travel then you can claim the mileage allowances shown on page 53.

Technical and other books on your firm's products or services. It may be advisable to obtain a letter from your employer confirming that this expenditure is necessary for your job.

Use of your home as an office. If you have to do a lot of work for your employer at home, and use a specific room for this purpose, you ought to claim an allowance based on a proportion of total upkeep, e.g. rent, light, heat, insurance, cleaning, repairs to furniture, etc. If such a room is used *wholly* for work a proportion of the council tax may be claimable, but some capital gains tax may be payable on the sale of the house. Such a claim should be made under the 'other expenses' box on the Employment sheet in your tax return.

Telephone – part of your own telephone bill covering calls to customers, etc., if that part is not paid by your employer.

Gifts to customers paid for by yourself which do not cost more than £10 per customer per year and which advertise your firm's products or services. (The gift must not be of food, drink, tobacco – or a voucher!)

Fees, subscriptions, journals and publications essential to your employment or profession.

Travelling expenses

You are able to claim travelling expenses as a tax deduction against your income provided the journeys were not repetitive, i.e. from your home to a permanent place of work. This means that if your work takes you to many different locations, even if you start from home each day, then such expenses can be claimed. However, if you routinely visit a different office or branch each day of the week you may have more than one permanent workplace. The tax legislation is complicated, but where a site-based employee is working for more than 24 months at that workplace, it will be regarded as permanent and travelling expenses from home to site will *not* be allowed for tax.

Incidental overnight expenses

Miscellaneous personal expenses up to £5 a night paid by the employer whilst away from home on business in the UK (£10 a night abroad) are tax free.

Interest payments

If you have to borrow money to buy equipment (e.g. car, computer) necessary for your job, then the interest can be claimed as an expense against your income. Interest on a bank overdraft and credit cards is not allowable.

Employees earning £8,500 or more, and directors

All employees whose earnings, expenses *and potential benefits* are at the rate of £8,500 a year or more, and most directors regardless of their earnings or expenses, have their benefits and expenses reported to the tax office by their employer.

The employer has to do this by law and fills in the notoriously complicated Form P11D which is sent to the tax office. There is a legal obligation for all employers to give their employees copies of these forms by 6 July which will be a help in checking your tax.

You might receive a letter from your tax office asking for details of these expenses, and you must then convince them that you did not receive any personal benefit or, if you did, obtain their agreement on the proportion of the expenses to be disallowed. You will pay tax on this proportion.

Sometimes an employer can arrange with the tax inspector to get a 'dispensation' making it unnecessary for him to complete certain parts of Form P11D, in which case the employee does not need to include such expense in the tax return.

The major conditions for a dispensation are normally that the reimbursement of expenses is closely supervised and it is obvious that the expenses themselves are easily justifiable (e.g. travelling and subsistence expenses for a representative).

Even if a dispensation is granted, the expenses still have to be taken into account in deciding if an employee earns £8,500 or more.

An employer may also make an arrangement to meet the tax liability on behalf of employees in respect of certain benefits. This is known as a PAYE Settlement Agreement and may cover items such as Christmas gifts, awards and shared benefits.

CHAPTER SEVEN

Your 2000 Tax Return Income from property and investments etc.

This chapter deals with income from land and property, and dividends and interest from investments, trusts and maintenance.

Assets held in joint names

If a husband and wife have income from an asset held in joint names it is divided equally when filling in tax returns. If the ownership is not held equally, then you should ask the tax office for Form 17 on which you can jointly declare the actual ownership split. You then enter the amounts accordingly in your tax returns. Such declaration takes effect from the date it is made provided the form is sent to the tax office within 60 days.

Property income

The tax return supplementary pages *Land and Property* cover all aspects of property income (see page 30).

If a *husband and wife* own a property that is let, the tax office will assume that any income from these assets is divided equally.

You should enter in your tax return one half of the income and expenses, writing in the word 'Joint' to indicate to the tax office that it is a joint holding.

If the ownership is *not* held equally, then refer above as to the action you should take.

For the purposes of income tax, all income from property in the UK, including furnished, unfurnished and holiday lettings, is taxable on the same 'commercial' basis as any other business (see page 100) – that is that expenditure is allowable against profits if it is wholly and exclusively for business purposes. ('Rent-a-room' relief continues to be available however.)

Listed on the next page are details of expenses that you might be able to claim against any property income you may have.

Property expenses

If you receive rents from a property which you let furnished or unfurnished you can claim the following expenses, if applicable:

Rent paid and water rates

General maintenance and repairs of the property, garden and furniture and fittings

Costs of agents for letting, and collecting rents

Insurance, including insurance premium tax

Interest payable on a loan to purchase, or improve, investment property (but see page 66 for restrictions)

Charges for preparing inventories

Legal fees – on renewing a tenancy agreement, for leases of not more than 50 years, or on the initial grant of a lease not exceeding 21 years

Accountancy fees to prepare and agree your income

Costs of collecting rents which could in some cases include your travelling expenses to and from the property

Costs of services e.g. porters, cleaners, security

Wear and tear allowance for furniture and fittings; generally 10 per cent of the basic rent receivable. As an alternative, the cost of renewals may be claimed

Council tax

Rent-A-Room Relief

Owner occupiers and tenants who let furnished accommodation in their own or main home are able to receive rent up to £4,250 a year exempt from income tax. Make sure you tell your insurers and your mortgage company, if you enter into a rent-a-room arrangement.

If rent exceeds these limits, you have the option of either paying the excess without any deduction for allowable expenses, or calculating any profit made (gross rents less actual allowable expenses) and paying tax on that profit in the normal way.

An individual's exempt limit is halved if, at any time during a tax year, someone else received income from letting in the same property.

Interest from savings and investments

You need to differentiate between interest that has had tax deducted and that which has been paid gross.

If you have joint savings or investments only include in the tax return your share of the income.

Show all your income from National Savings, but exclude the first £70 interest earned on any ordinary account because this is tax-free. You do not have to include interest from National Savings certificates as that too is tax-free.

Remember to include National Savings Capital Bonds under this section of the tax return – the interest is taxed on an annual basis, even though it is not actually received until the Bond is repaid after five years. Include details of FIRST Option Bonds separately.

If you are doubtful about excluding any income, the notes that come with your tax return have lists of claims to include and items to exclude in the totals in your tax return.

If your deposit, savings or investment account interest is not paid to you at regular intervals, it is wise to send the book into the society for interest to be entered in each tax year. There is no need to enter interest from SAYE accounts as it is not taxable.

Dividends from shares in UK companies

Enter the amounts that you actually received and the amount of tax credits as shown on your dividend slips. The date on the dividend slip is considered as being the date receivable for tax return purposes. Show income from most unit trusts here, including the income that was reinvested in further units instead of being paid direct to you. The treatment of tax credits is shown on page 87.

Scrip dividends should also be included here. The dividend statement should show 'the appropriate amount in cash' which is the dividend.

Accrued income securities

Where fixed interest securities are sold or purchased and the contract note either includes accrued income charges or deducts accrued income reliefs, then these figures must be included in box 13.3 if the charges exceed reliefs, and deducted from the figure in box 10.4 if the reliefs exceed the charges.

Income from trusts and settlements, etc.

Normally most estates of deceased persons will have a professional executor or administrator. They should provide you with a form R185 which will identify payments made to you and any tax deducted. If you do not receive this form, then seek advice as to the details you need to include in your tax return.

The tax return has supplementary pages covering Trusts and settlements (see page 35).

You may be able to claim tax back in respect of income from discretionary trusts (see page 88) if you are not a higher rate tax payer.

In the supplementary pages of the tax return you also have to give details of settlements made, for although capital or income may not have been received by you, it may be considered by the tax office to be your income for tax purposes. The most common example would be income from gifts you may have made to minor children. (See also page 78).

Children's income

If you have made gifts to your children who are under the age of 18, then the whole of any income resulting from that gift should be included in your tax return as savings income if it amounts to more than £100 gross. (See also page 78.)

Maintenance or alimony received

Maintenance or alimony received is not taxable unless it is paid under arrangements which were first made prior to 15 March 1988. There is also an exemption of £1,970 for 1999–2000, but *all* maintenance payments are exempt from tax as from 6 April 2000.

State the gross amount you have received under a court order or agreement for the maintenance of yourself or your children. Most maintenance agreements are paid without tax having been deducted. If tax has been deducted, clearly state this in the additional information box on page 8 of the return. Voluntary payments are not taxable and should not be shown. (See also page 70.)

CHAPTER EIGHT

Your 2000 Tax Return
Interest and other payments
allowed for tax

This chapter covers **payments** made by you which may be allowed for tax relief and should be shown on your tax return.

These could include interest charges on loans, covenants and donations to charities, maintenance payments, and payments for vocational training, tax efficient investments, and payments to trade unions and friendly societies.

Vocational training (VTR)

Payments for qualifying vocational training courses were eligible for tax relief. The relief was given by the basic rate tax being deducted from the course fees. You could get this deduction even if you were not liable to tax. (Ask your tax office for leaflet IR119 for more information.)

Higher rate tax relief was withdrawn from 6 April 1999.

VTR is abolished in 2000–2001 and Individual Learning Accounts can now be set up, giving lump sums for committed education and training schemes.

The Government will commit £150 for each account holder if the individual commits a minimum of £25; any contributions from employers will be free of tax and national insurance for employees.

Interest on loans for the purchase of private residence

For 1999–2000 interest was allowed for tax on total loans not exceeding £30,000 if the loan was for the purchase of a main residence or land on which to build one, and was in the UK or Republic of Ireland.

The tax relief was restricted to 10 per cent. The relief is withdrawn completely from April 2000.

There is no relief for overdraft interest, nor for interest on loans for improvements taken out after 5 April 1988, but note that if the improvement is a barn conversion, whilst you cannot get tax relief on the loan interest, you *can* reclaim any VAT on materials used for building.

Interest was allowed for tax on loans taken out *prior* to 6 April 1988 if the loan was to improve a house, or buy a house that was occupied rent-free by a dependent relative who, by being incapacitated by old age or infirmity was being maintained by you, or to buy a house for a former or separated husband or wife. The amount of such a loan, however, counted towards the £30,000 limit referred to above.

The £30,000 limit applied to the *property* regardless of the number of borrowers. It was possible for several residents each to have a mortgage on the same house, but relief on the interest was still restricted to a maximum total loan amount of £30,000.

The maximum relief each owner of a property could have was '£30,000 divided by the number of borrowers'. If an owner was not utilising his full portion the difference could be transferred for tax relief purposes to another owner of the same property.

Tax procedure on interest payments

For house loans that had been approved by the tax office, then, under the 'Miras' system, you were allowed to deduct tax at the reduced rate of 10 per cent from the interest at the time it was paid, up to a maximum loan amount of £30,000. This tax relief was withdrawn from 6 April 2000.

'Miras' stands for Mortgage Interest Relief at Source. You were allowed to deduct the tax even if your total income was at a level that would not normally be liable to tax. The interest on the proportion of any loan over £30,000 had to be paid gross.

You do not have to give details of mortgage interest covered by 'Miras' on your tax return as you will already have received the tax relief by deducting tax from the payment.

Married couples and mortgage interest

Regardless of whether the property or the mortgage is in the wife's or husband's name, then provided it is the couple's main residence, mortgage interest paid to 5 April 2000 and up to a maximum loan of £30,000 can be allocated between the couple whichever way they choose to give the most beneficial tax advantage.

You can also vary the ratios from year to year by filling in Form 15 within 12 months from 31 January following the end of the tax year. (This only applies to mortgage interest; generally other reliefs are only available to the person who actually pays for the expense.)

It should be beneficial to consider apportioning mortgage interest relief in the following circumstances:

(a) if the loan is outside the 'Miras' rules (see above), ensure that the person who claims the tax relief is liable to tax.

(b) if you are aged 65 or over, allocate the interest to avoid the age allowance earnings restriction (see page 92).

Bridging loans

Until 5 April 2000 interest on bridging loans was allowable for tax for up to 12 months (possibly extended at your tax inspector's discretion) on up to £30,000 in addition to any maximum new borrowing.

Borrowers could continue to get relief on the loan interest on their old property, for up to one year, provided it was put up for sale, even if you did not take a new loan. In order to alleviate negative equity problems, lenders had been able to keep an old loan in existence, rather than redeeming it and advancing a new loan, without the borrower losing entitlement to mortgage interest relief.

Interest paid on loans to buy an investment property

Property investments are assessed on the same basis as any other business (see page 100) – that is, that expenditure is allowable against profits if it is wholly and exclusively for business purposes.

The interest rules also extend to overseas properties as well as those in the UK.

Refer to page 30 as to what has to be entered in the *Land and Property* section of the return in box 15.2.

Interest on other loans

Having dealt with interest on loans for the purchase of property, there are other types of loans (called 'qualifying loans') the interest on which is also allowed for tax.

They include loans to buy shares or lend to:

(a) A closely controlled trading company where you own more than 5 per cent of the company's shares, or, if less, have worked for the greater part of your time in the management of the company – such interest is not allowed for tax if the shares qualified for tax relief under the Business Expansion Scheme or Enterprise Investment Scheme.

(b) A partnership

(c) Certain annuities (see below)

(d) A co-operative, provided you work for it full-time

Loans to pay inheritance tax or buy plant or machinery for business use also qualify. (See page 42 – box 15.3.)

Interest on loans to purchase an annuity

This relief was abolished for *new* loans taken out with effect from 9 March 1999.

For old loans, such interest is allowed for tax if the person buying the annuity is aged 65 or over, where the loan is secured on that individual's main residence in the UK or the Republic of Ireland and the loan does not exceed £30,000.

Tax at the basic rate may be deducted from the interest at the time of payment, provided the loan does not exceed this limit (see also page 96).

Retirement annuity payments and personal pensions

Refer to page 130 for a summary of the tax efficient opportunities that can arise from pension planning.

Hire purchase and credit card interest

You cannot claim relief on this type of interest unless you pay it in connection with your business activities.

Interest on overdue tax

This cannot be claimed as a deduction for tax purposes (see page 89).

Private medical insurance

Tax relief on payments for private medical insurance for the over 60s was abolished in respect of annual contracts made or renewed on or after 2 July 1997.

Tax relief was given by basic rate tax being deducted from the premium paid for existing contracts until they expire.

Maintenance and alimony payments

You cannot get tax relief for UK maintenance payments unless there is a legal obligation to make them, for example under a separation deed or court order.

A person making maintenance payments should not deduct tax from them but will get tax relief either through a PAYE coding or a tax assessment. The maximum payment that can qualify for tax relief is £1,970 at 10 per cent for 1999–2000 (£1,900 at 15 per cent for 1998–99) – any excess does not qualify for relief and the relief ceases if the person receiving it remarries.

This allowance is abolished for all maintenance payments from 6 April 2000 except where one of the couple is 65 or over on that date.

Note that there were special rules and reliefs affecting maintenance payments to adults, and to children, if they were paid under a legally binding agreement made before 15 March 1988, or a court order applied for on or before that date but in place by 30 June 1988. In certain circumstances you could benefit by making an election to transfer to the current tax relief levels.

Tax relief on any maintenance payments for the benefit of children ceased when they reached the age of 21 or 5 April 2000, whichever was earlier.

Ask your tax office for explanatory leaflet IR93.

Venture capital trusts and enterprise investment scheme

It is in the *Reliefs* section of your tax return that you need to state details of the investments – see page 128 for tax advantages.

Covenanted payments to charities

Covenants are used to transfer income in a tax efficient way to charities; to be effective for income tax purposes they must be for more than three years.

You deduct tax from a payment under a deed of covenant at the basic rate.

Payments under covenant to charities are deductible in calculating higher rate tax, even though only basic rate tax will have been deducted when the payment was made (see also page 130).

You should enter on your tax return the name of the person or body to whom you make the payment, and the net amount paid after deduction of tax.

Gift aid donations to charity

This scheme applies to single gifts made by individuals and charities. The minimum gift was £250 up to 5 April 2000 but this minimum limit has now been abolished. Gifts are made net of basic rate tax and charities are able to claim repayment of the tax.

Higher rate tax relief is also available to the giver where applicable.

The Millennium gift aid scheme has been set up to receive donations to support education and anti-poverty projects in the world's poorest countries. Gifts made to this scheme qualify for tax relief if made between 31 July 1998 and 31 December 2000, provided they are over £100 (gifts by instalments once they reach £100 are also eligible).

Payments to trade unions, friendly societies

If you make compulsory payments to provide annuities for widows and orphans where relief is not given by your employer or if part of your trade union subscription relates to a pension, insurance or funeral benefit, or you have a friendly society policy providing sickness and death benefits, then you can claim tax relief on one half of the payments.

CHAPTER NINE

Personal Allowances

A tax allowance is not a payment; it is the amount of income you can receive without paying tax. Apart from the personal allowance, all allowances are claimed by filling in a tax return. The allowances for 2000–2001 as announced in the Budget are as follows:

Personal allowances

Age as at 5 April 2000	Personal Allowance £	Married Couple's Allowance £
Under 65 years of age	4,385	Nil
Between 65 and 74	*5,790	†5,185
75 and over	*6,050	†5,255

*These age-related allowances are however restricted if your income is over £17,000. For every £2 of income above this limit your allowance is reduced by £1, but no taxpayer can get less than the basic personal allowance of £4,385.
†Relief is restricted to 10 per cent.

The married couples' allowance

The married couple's allowance was abolished from 6 April 2000 except for couples where either the husband or wife was aged 65 or more on that date.

This can be claimed by a married man living with his wife, or, if permanently separated but still married to her, if wholly maintaining her by voluntary payments.

A wife can claim one half of the married couple's allowance, or indeed the whole of the allowance, if her husband agrees.

Ask your tax office for Form 18 but this has to be submitted before the start of the tax year to which it relates.

If it is preferred that the husband gets the whole of the married couple's allowance then there is no need to take any action.

Married couples – transfer of surplus allowances

A husband can transfer to his wife any unused married couple's allowance and sometimes transitionally, unused personal allowance. This is fully explained in Chapter 10.

Additional personal allowance/single parent allowance

This allowance is completely abolished from 6 April 2000 for everyone. Prior to this date, if you were a one-parent family, or were looking after children because your husband or wife was incapacitated throughout the year, you were entitled to an additional allowance of £1,970 at 10 per cent for 1999–2000.

This allowance was given if your child was living with you and was under 16, or if older and was receiving full time education or on a training course for at least two years. It was also given for a child under 18 who was not your child but who was living with and maintained by you. An unmarried couple living together as man and wife could only claim £1,970 between them.

Widows

Widows were entitled to an additional tax allowance of £1,970 at 10 per cent for 1999–2000 in the year of bereavement and any unused married couple's allowance for the year of the husband's death could also be claimed. The additional personal allowance was also available if applicable (see above).

This widow's bereavement allowance was abolished from 6 April 2000 but will be available in 2000–2001 at £2,000 to a woman widowed in 1999–2000 if she does not remarry before 6 April 2000.

Blind person's allowance

A registered blind person is entitled to an extra tax allowance of £1,380 for 1999–2000 and £1,400 for 2000–2001. This allowance is also claimable by blind persons in the year preceding the year in which they were officially registered as blind if, at the end of the previous year, evidence was then available to support the eventual registration. The allowance is transferable to a husband or wife even if he or she is not blind.

If you require help with a Braille version of the tax return or notes telephone the Inland Revenue on 01274 539646.

CHAPTER TEN

Family tax matters

Whether you are starting your first job, getting married, saving money or working on your own, you cannot escape the tax inspector.

Many people experience great difficulty in claiming repayments back from their tax office for one reason or another.

The secret behind dealing with any tax claim is to comply with 'the system'. The whole of our tax system revolves around forms and the written word!

Either telephone your tax office, or call in or write and ask for the correct form, depending upon your circumstances – fill it in and send it to your tax office, in order to start the ball rolling. Always state your tax reference number.

If you are taxed under PAYE write to the tax inspector who deals with your employer's PAYE. If you are self-employed you will deal with the inspector who covers your business address.

Here are some practical steps to bear in mind:

Starting work

(a) PAYE

You will need a code number (see page 81).

Your employer will fill in a form P46 and give this to you for signature. You then select which of the statements A, B or C applies to you and complete the rest of the form.

If, however, you decide to work for yourself, or in partnership with someone else, you will eventually have to fill in a tax return on which you will claim your allowances and declare your income. Thus the PAYE system will not apply to you and all you need to do is to tell your tax office when your business commences.

(b) National Insurance contributions

National Insurance contributions are levied depending on how much you earn. See Chapter 15 for further details.

Changes in allowances and deductions

Most tax allowances are not given to you automatically – they have to be claimed and the claim must be supported by the right information.

The more common instances of changes in allowances and deductions are covered in this chapter.

Getting married

For 1999–2000 both husband and wife will each receive the personal allowance, with the husband getting the married couple's allowance only for each month of the marriage – but see page 72.

Working families' tax credit

This was introduced from 5 October 1999 and replaces Family Credit. It also incorporates the childcare tax credit scheme.

Couples or lone parents who have one or more children, where either partner works over 16 hours a week and have savings of £8,000 or less can apply for this tax credit.

The tax credits were administered by the Department of Social Security until 5 April 2000 but the Inland Revenue tax offices have now taken over responsibility.

You should apply to your tax office for application forms and full details.

The table on page 140 gives the rates for 2000–2001.

Disabled person's tax credit

This was introduced at the same time as the above and is similarly administered by the Inland Revenue. It replaced the disability working allowance.

Unemployed husband

For 1999–2000 if a husband's income is insufficient to cover his allowable mortgage interest, then the unused balance may be transferred to his wife if she has any income in her own right. Ask your tax office for Form 15.

You may also claim for any unused married couple's allowance in 1999–2000 to be transferred to your wife where this is to your advantage – ask for Claim Form 575. There is a box to tick, making this request, in your tax return. This allowance was abolished from 6 April 2000 except for those couples where either the husband or wife was aged 65 or over on or before 5 April 2000.

It is also possible in certain isolated circumstances for the husband to transfer his unused personal allowance to his wife.

Ask the tax office to give you details of how to qualify for this transfer.

What should married couples do to benefit fully from independent taxation?

(a) As a wife gets a personal allowance in her own right, it will be wasted if she does not work and has no income at all – it cannot be transferred to her husband.

If possible, therefore, her husband should transfer investments into her name so that she gets income to offset against her personal allowance. Ensure that such income is either paid gross by choosing an appropriate investment (see page 124) or, if savings are in a bank or building society account, ensuring that you fill in form R85. If you ask your tax office for leaflet IR110 you get explanatory notes as well as the appropriate form.

(b) If a husband or wife is paying tax at the higher rate (40 per cent) then, again, transferring some income-producing assets between them would be beneficial if one partner is on the lower or basic rate tax band, or is not using all of the personal allowance.

Sometimes a husband (or wife) may be reluctant to transfer cash or assets in case they may be 'spent'. One solution is to transfer an asset into joint ownership as 'tenants in common'. Whilst the original owner could retain, say, a 95 per cent share, the Inland Revenue would treat the income as being split 50:50, if no declaration of actual ownership is made. In some cases it may be beneficial to make a declaration of ownership in which case ask the tax office for Form 17 *before* the start of a tax year (you cannot backdate such a request).

(c) Married couples aged 65 and over should similarly check that their tax affairs are organised as above, because the higher personal allowance, which each of them gets in their own right, is reduced if their incomes exceed certain limits (see page 91).

(d) Ensure that tax relief on covenants is not lost (see page 130).

(e) If at all practicable, ensure that your investments are allocated between you or held in joint names so that you can each take full benefit of the capital gains exemption limit when investments are sold.

(f) A wife who is 65 on or before 6 April 2000 can reclaim one half, or the whole, of the married couple's allowance. Refer to page 72 to see what you need to do.

Raising a family

As soon as your baby is born ask at your local Benefits Agency office for a child benefit claim form. Complete this and return it to them with the birth certificate.

Child benefit is normally payable to the mother and collectable each week at your local post office or it can be paid direct into your bank account each month. The benefit is tax-free. This benefit may also be claimed by one-parent families and for adopted children. Statutory maternity pay may be available from your employer.

Child care facilities

Employees can benefit from the use of child care facilities provided by their employer without incurring a tax charge on that benefit.

To qualify for the exemption:

(a) the child must be under 18,

(b) the premises must not be domestic premises,

(c) the premises must be provided by the employer (or a group of employers or a local authority) with each employer(s) being responsible for finance and management,

(d) paid for directly by the employer (in other words, cash allowances, vouchers or reimbursement would not qualify).

The Budget confirmed that there would be no National Insurance contributions levied on child care facilities provided by an employer.

Children's income

Each child is an individual taxpayer entitled to his or her own personal allowance. Parents are not taxable on a child's casual earnings nor on income arising on gifts from relatives. However, if you give cash or property to your children, any income over £100 a year arising from such gifts is treated as your income for tax purposes until your child is 18.

The only way in which parents can transfer larger sums to their children without continuing to pay tax on the income from those assets is by setting up an irrecoverable trust which can accumulate income until the child is 18. However, if income is paid direct to the child before then, it will be taxed as the income of the parent.

On the other hand, a child can receive, or benefit from, income provided by a relative, either by the gift of investments or by setting up a trust which pays out income for the child's education and maintenance.

In these cases you should ask your tax office for Form 232 (included in R40) on which to declare your child's income and, if the income has had tax deducted before receipt, for example, trust income, interest, etc., claim a tax repayment in respect of the child's personal allowance.

Students

Earnings from holiday jobs will often have PAYE tax deducted. Ask your employer for form P38(S) which, when completed and returned to him, will enable payment to be made without tax deductions if you do not earn above the personal allowance for the year.

One parent families

In addition to the personal allowance and the child benefit, a one-parent family could claim an additional personal allowance prior to 6 April 2000 (see page 73). Ask any tax office for leaflet IR92.

In addition, of course, the normal social security benefits may be claimed.

Divorce or separation

In the year of permanent separation, a husband who was 65 on or before 6 April 2000 can claim the full married couple's allowance for that year (unless an election has been made to apportion it), although this can be transferred to his wife if the husband's income is insufficient to use it all.

See page 70 for the tax treatment of maintenance payments.

Death of a wife or husband

After the death of a wife and provided the husband or wife was 65 on or before 6 April 2000, the husband will continue to get the married couple's allowance for that year (excluding any part that the wife may have used against her income) plus his own personal allowance.

Following the death of a husband aged 65 on or before 6 April 2000, a wife can claim any unused married couple's allowance plus the widow's bereavement allowance (see page 73) and her own personal allowance.

The widow's bereavement allowance can also be claimed in the tax year *following* bereavement, unless the widow has remarried. (Widowers cannot claim a similar allowance.)

Ceasing employment

Permanently: Send Form P45, which your employer will have given you, to your tax office whose district is shown on the form. Also write a letter confirming that you have either retired, ceased working, or have become self-employed, and claim any tax repayment.

Temporarily: When you change employment or are made redundant, and there is a gap between one job and the next, you will need to hand in Form P45 when you sign on to claim benefits. The Benefits Agency will advise you on the proportion of your jobseeker's allowance that is taxable and will deal with any tax refund due at the end of the tax year. Alternatively, if you are not entitled to benefits, send in your P45 to your tax office telling them you are temporarily unemployed.

If you do not start a new job by the following 5 April, check your total income and tax, as shown in Chapter 12, to see if there is a repayment or underpayment of tax due.

Making a will

It is important to make a will for it will ensure in the event of your death the things that you own, your house, investments, etc., will pass to those whom you wish should have them.

It is not expensive, or time-consuming, to make a will – contact your local solicitor for a short meeting.

If you do not make a will, handling your estate is more difficult and the law will distribute your assets under the rules of intestacy.

Are you claiming your tax refund?

The Inland Revenue estimates that around seven million people are due tax refunds and are not claiming them.

There are broadly three main categories of people who should consider claiming tax refunds:

(a) Shareholders

Many people, including children, who are not taxpayers because their income does not exceed their tax allowances, hold shares and receive dividends on which tax has been deducted in the form of a tax credit. This credit can be claimed back from the Inland Revenue for periods of up to six years prior to 5 April 1999.

However, the tax credit cannot be reclaimed in these circumstances after 6 April 1999 and alternative investments that pay interest gross should be considered.

(b) Pensioners

The above comments also apply to pensioners but, in addition, many pensioners whose income is less than their age-related allowance may also be receiving additional pensions and other interest on which tax has been deducted. Again, many will be entitled to tax refunds (see Chapter 12).

(c) Savers with building society and bank accounts

Interest paid by building societies and banks will have had tax deducted from it at the savings rate (20 per cent) before it is paid to you.

If your total income is less than your personal allowance (see page 72) as will often be the case for children, wives who are not earning and pensioners on low income, then you should claim that tax back.

Even if your total income does exceed your personal allowance, with the starting rate of tax at only 10 per cent since 6 April 1999 you can claim the difference between the two rates.

If your total income is less than your personal allowance ask your bank or building society for form R85, fill it in (you will need your national insurance number) and return it to them. Once they have this form, they can pay you interest in future without tax having been deducted.

To claim a tax refund

Write to any tax office asking for leaflet IR110. This gives you some helpful information and, in particular, the leaflet contains a form for you to fill in and return to your tax office requesting a tax refund. (See page 88 for further details.)

CHAPTER ELEVEN

PAYE and code numbers

The Pay As You Earn system was introduced to enable every employee to pay tax by weekly or monthly instalments rather than in one hefty amount at the end of the tax year. By law your employer has to deduct PAYE tax and NI from your earnings.

How does an employer know how much to deduct?

You are allocated a code number by your tax office, and your employer uses this to find out the tax to be deducted from your earnings.

The code is a shortened method of defining your total tax-free pay (usually the total of your allowances), but in fact the last figure is omitted. The code effectively spreads your allowances evenly throughout the tax year.

Your code number actually tells you how much you can earn before you start paying tax, for example, a code 512H means that you are married and start paying tax at basic rate after you have earned £5,120 (£98.46 each week).

A Notice of Tax Code is sent to you if your code changes; it details your allowances, benefits, untaxed income, etc, and shows your code number. If you do not receive one, you can request a copy from your tax office.

Your employer is also advised of the new code but is not given the details as to how it is compiled *so he cannot check it for you.*

You should make sure that all allowances due to you are included and be sure your code is amended if your allowances alter during the year.

The higher your code, the lower your tax, unless you have a code with a 'K' prefix.

What do the letters mean?
The letter shown after your code defines your status e.g.for 2000–2001 L – basic personal allowance entitlement; H – personal allowance plus basic married couple's allowance or additional personal allowance and a basic rate taxpayer; (A for higher rate taxpayer); P – single pensioner under 75; V – married pensioner with full married couple's allowance and basic rate taxpayer. Y is

the tax code for the personal allowance for those aged 75 or over. Letter T is used in most other cases but you can also request it be used if you do not wish your employer to know your status. OT means that no allowances have been given – this is often used if you haven't sent in a tax return for a long time or your tax affairs are very complicated.

Other codes are: NT – no tax payable; BR – all earnings to be taxed at the basic rate; D – to be taxed at the higher rate.

Sometimes your taxable benefits will exceed your allowances – for example, if you are taxed on car and fuel benefits and private health benefits, or owe back tax. In these cases a K code is used so that your employer can recoup this tax on behalf of the tax office.

The tax office may *estimate* any likely taxable benefits for the 2000–2001 tax year and will probably base them on the latest available figures on their files, which could be quite old if you haven't sent in a tax return for the last couple of years.

You need to check the figures on your notice of code number carefully. If the estimates are excessive write to your tax office requesting a code change – be sure to quote your NI number and the reference. If the estimates are much too low, bear in mind that if you take no action you may end up with a large underpayment at the end of the tax year.

Check your code number

A typical Notice of Tax Code will contain your name and address, tax office address, your tax reference number and your National Insurance number.

On the left hand side will be your allowances. These will certainly include your personal allowance to which may be added items such as the married couple's allowance, allowable expenses, professional subscriptions, etc.

The married couple's allowance, additional personal allowance and relief for maintenance payments were withdrawn from 6 April 2000 but the married couple's allowance and maintenance relief continue for those couples where either the husband or wife was 65 on or before 5 April 2000.

Widow's bereavement allowance is also withdrawn except for women widowed in 1999–2000.

On the right hand side will be the deductions, typically company car benefit, fuel benefit, other benefits and miscellaneous income on which you have not paid PAYE, and possibly an allowance restriction (see below).

Deducting the right hand column from the left hand column will give you your net allowances; your code will be identified on the form.

On the reverse of the notice of tax code will be explanations showing when your new code will come into operation.

Ideally, the figures making up your code number should agree with the figures in your tax return.

If your code is incorrect, it is more than likely that your previous year's code was also wrong, so that any overpayment of tax is accumulating.

Allowance restriction

On the Notices of Code for the **year to 5 April 2000** the basic married couple's allowance of £1,970 may be shown in full on the left hand side, even though relief is only available at 10 per cent.

In order to adjust this (and provided you have no age income restriction), the figures on the right hand side are likely to be £1,110 for basic rate taxpayers and £1,475 for higher rate tax payers.

There will be similar figures. if you are eligible.for the widow's bereavement allowance or maintenance payment relief.

The figures for the year to 5 April 2001 are likely to be £1,090 for basic rate taxpayers and £1,500 for higher rate taxpayers. Similar adjustments will be required in both years where you are entitled to the higher amounts of married couple's allowance.

CHAPTER TWELVE

How to check your tax

At the end of the tax year you should check to see if you have paid the correct tax. Those who are self-employed should be more aware during the year as to their tax affairs and Chapter 14 specifically deals with this.

This chapter is primarily for employees on PAYE, although it will be of interest to all taxpayers as many of the circumstances are not confined to those on PAYE.

At the end of every tax year your employer must give you a Form P60 which will show how much you have earned in the tax year and, more importantly, how much tax you have paid.

If you receive benefits (company car, health insurance, etc.) you will also receive a Form P11D (see page 61) which will identify these.

You should immediately check for yourself whether the amount of tax you have paid is correct.

Follow these steps in order to check last year's tax:

(a) Add up your total earnings and benefits in the year and deduct your expenses claimed (e.g. any allowable mortgage or loan interest paid without tax having been deducted, pension contributions and other expenses outlined in Chapter 6) to arrive at your 'net earnings'. Just because you are on PAYE does not mean you cannot claim expenses (see page 59).

(b) List all the allowances which were due to you – refresh your memory by turning to page 139.

(c) Subtract the total of (b) from your 'net earnings' to arrive at the earnings on which you start paying tax. Rates of tax are given on page 139.

This will then give you the total tax you should have paid under PAYE, but don't forget if you have income from savings this will also need to be considered.

If this total tax figure – in (c) – is less than that stated on your P60 form you have paid too much tax. Write immediately to your tax office pointing this out and then claim a refund. If you have not paid enough tax, either you or the tax inspector has made a mistake!

If you have paid insufficient tax you are under a legal obligation to send in a tax return so that any outstanding tax can be calculated and paid.

The tax office may also adjust your code number so that you do not underpay tax in the following year.

Here are examples showing you how to check your tax.

Here is an example of checking your tax for the year ended 5 April 2000:

Michael, who is married, is employed and had a salary of £25,300 from which his employer had deducted a pension contribution of £750. His employer provided him with a company car and fuel.

He did some freelance work at home which, after expenses, gave him £545.

His tax liability can be summarised as follows:

Total wages per P60 form (£25,300)	
less pension contribution £750	£24,550
Casual earnings	545
Use of company car and fuel benefit, say	3,160
Total earnings for the year	28,255
Deduct: Expenses claimed	195
'Net earnings'	28,060
Deduct: Personal allowance	4,335
Earnings on which tax is payable	£23,725
Tax payable £ 1,500 at 10% £ 150.00	
£22,225 at 23% £5,111.75	5,261.75
Deduct: Married couple's allowance £1,970 at 10%	197.00
Tax due	5,064.75
Less: Tax paid under PAYE as shown on form P60, say	5,200.00
Amount of tax to be claimed back	£ 135.25

It has been assumed that any mortgage interest paid was under the MIRAS scheme, i.e. tax has been deducted from payments made.

Assuming that the above are the figures you have declared in your 2000 tax return, then the statement you get from the tax office should agree with your tax calculations and also confirm that a refund is due. If you have adjustments in your tax code to collect underpayments for 1999–2000 or earlier tax years, contact your tax office for further advice.

In the above example it had been assumed that Michael received no interest or dividends from savings. If he had received such income then the tax system becomes more complicated because tax on savings income is taxed differently (see below).

The tax office uses a different method

The way in which the above statement was prepared is the normal and simplest way, and the method most professional accountants would use.

Unfortunately, our tax system always makes things as complicated as possible and the statements you receive from the tax office will present the details in a different format. They tend to work backwards, allocating income against tax bands.

However, the net result should be the same and if it is not and you cannot see at a glance why there is a difference, then write to your tax office and enclose a copy of *your* workings so they can identify the problems.

Tax on savings income

In the Budget review of November 1999 it was announced that the starting rate of 10 per cent would *include* savings income (other than dividends) as well as earnings and this would be backdated to 6 April 1999.

Once the £1,500 band has been used up then the savings are taxed at 20 per cent for basic rate taxpayers and 40 per cent for higher rate taxpayers.

Here are two examples to show how this is calculated:

Example one (basic rate taxpayer)

In 1999–2000 John has a taxable income, after allowances, of £5,000, of which £500 is the gross amount of interest.

He will pay tax on the first £1,500 (incl. interest) at 10 per cent	£150
The balance of £3,500 at the basic rate of 23 per cent	805
Tax payable	£955

If tax at 20 per cent had been deducted from the interest before it was paid to John, then the total amount of the tax payable, £955 would be reduced by the amount of tax deducted from the income.

If John's income from savings had come from dividends instead of interest, the gross amount of the dividend would have been liable to tax at 10 per cent in addition to the starting rate tax band of £1,500.

Example two (higher rate taxpayer)

In 1999–2000 Jane has a taxable income, after allowances, of £30,000, of which £5,000 is the gross amount of interest. She will be liable for tax as follows:

	£
On her non-savings income	
£ 1,500 at 10 per cent	150
£23,500 at 23 per cent	5,405
£ 2,000 at 40 per cent	800
On her savings income	
£ 3,000 at 20 per cent	600
Tax payable	£6,955

If tax had been deducted from the interest before it was paid to Jane, then the total amount of the tax payable, £6,955 would be reduced by the amount of tax deducted from the interest.

As above, if Jane had also received dividend income of £2,000 the tax credit plus the net dividend would have been included in the calculations and charged to tax at a rate of 32.5 per cent. The tax credit would be deducted from the tax payable.

Tax credits on dividends

Dividends are normally paid net of tax and are accompanied by a tax credit which can be deducted from your tax liability. Prior to 6 April 1999 the tax credit was 20 per cent. After that date it was reduced to 10 per cent and non-taxpayers and PEP holders were no longer able to claim a repayment of tax credits if their taxable income was below the tax threshold (that is, their gross income less allowances and reliefs take them below the figure at which tax is payable).

The higher rate of tax on dividend income is 32.5 per cent.

Example	**Prior to 5 April 1999** £		**Since 6 April 1999** £
UK dividend	80.00		80.00
Tax credit (20% of income)	20.00	(10%)	8.89
Income	100.00		88.89
Higher rate tax (40%)	40.00	(32.5%)	28.89
After tax income	£60.00		£60.00

As can be seen, the after-tax position for most higher-rate taxpayers is unaffected by the changes.

However, investment in shares for non-taxpayers obviously now becomes much less attractive (see pages 94 and 124).

Income tax repayment claim

If most of the income you receive has already been taxed (for example, interest) it is possible that you can claim back some tax.

Either fill in an ordinary tax return, or preferably ask for a repayment claim form (Form R40) telling your tax office in a covering letter that you think you are due a tax refund.

The Form R40 has space to claim expenses and deductions such as mortgage interest and personal allowances, in the same way as an ordinary tax return. You do not have to send dividend vouchers and certificates of deduction of tax in support of your claim. However, you should still keep the records as you may be asked to produce evidence at a later date.

Do not forget, when you sign the declaration, that there is another part of the form which you need to sign, which is your legal request for the actual repayment of tax to be made to you.

Tax repayment for the year 1999–2000

Joan, who is under 65, received earned income of £2,500 from which tax has not be deducted at source, plus net interest received of £2,000 (tax deducted £500).

Earned income		£2,500.00
Interest received	£2,000	
Tax deducted	500	2,500.00
		5,000.00
Deduct Personal allowance		4,335.00
		665.00
Tax liability: £665 × 10%		66.50
Tax deducted at source		500.00
Tax refund due		£ 433.50

If Joan had received net *dividend* income of £2,000 she would have a tax credit of £222 to set against her tax liability but the excess tax would not be repayable.

Tax demands in respect of 1999–2000 income

If your only income is taxed under PAYE, then it is unlikely that you will receive a tax return to fill in and, provided you have checked that the right amount of tax had been deducted, and your current PAYE code number is correct, then there is no need to contact your tax office.

If you have other income, or gains, in the year ended 5 April 2000 then you need to fill in a tax return. You should complete this and return it to your tax office before 30 September 2000.

The tax office will then send you a *self assessment tax calculation (Form SA302)* showing any sums due (or overpaid).

Should you wish to calculate your own tax then you have until 31 January 2001 to send in the tax return *together with* payment of any tax due.

Tax payments

If you generally receive income that does not have tax deducted from it when you receive it, then you have to pay one half of the estimated tax due on this income 'on account' during the year, and one half shortly after the end of the tax year. The same rules apply for income which is taxed at the basic or lower rate on which you are liable to higher rate tax.

In respect of income in the year ended 5 April 2000, one half 'on account' should have been paid on 31 January 2000 with the second half 'on account' due 31 July 2000. Any balancing payment arising after agreement of your tax liability for 1999–2000 will be due for payment on 31 January 2001 with the first half of your 'on account' payment for 2000–2001.

From time to time your tax office will send you *self assessment statements (Form SA300)* showing you the current position of your tax payments (or refunds).

If you disgree with it, ask for Form SA303 on which you can claim to reduce any payments on account.

Interest on late payments and repayments

The tax office will charge you interest on underpayments from the due date but will pay you interest called a repayment supplement and which is not taxable, on overpayments. The interest rate for repayment supplements is generally 4.5 per cent lower than that charged on late payment (see page 47).

CHAPTER THIRTEEN

Pensioners – your tax and your savings

This chapter applies only to those people who have reached the official retirement age of 65 for men and 60 for women. If you have elected for an earlier retirement you continue to be treated as a taxable individual and you cannot claim the tax concessions available to pensioners until the official retirement age. A married man is entitled to claim the retirement pension when he reaches 65. On the other hand, if a married woman reaches 60 before her husband is 65 she can only claim the pension if she has paid sufficient National Insurance contributions in her own right.

If the State pension is going to be your only income, then you can, and should, apply to your local Benefits Agency office and local council for various benefits to supplement your income.

A summary of social security benefits is shown on page 141.

What to do when you retire

If you have been paying PAYE you will receive a Form P45 from your employer. Send this to the tax office printed on the form with a letter stating that you have retired, giving the date on which you reached the age of 65, and stating that you are not intending to take further employment.

Should you later decide to work again, either full time or part time, you will have to ask your tax office for a new tax code.

If you have been self-employed, make sure that your tax returns are up to date, and tax liabilities agreed and inform your tax office of the details of any private pension you will receive.

Pensions

Most State pensions, including the old age pension and the widow's pension, are taxable, but the Government does not deduct the tax when you receive or collect it. If this State pension is your only source of income, however, then no tax will be payable as your personal allowance will more than cover this income. The war widow's pension is not taxable.

Many people nowadays receive not only the State pension but also a pension from a former employer, or an insurance company.

These additional pensions are normally taxed under PAYE and a code is applied which will have taken into account the amount you receive from the State pension before calculating the tax due.

If you are receiving income from two or more sources, it may appear that your tax burden is out of all proportion to the income being taxed. This may be because the tax inspector is deducting from one source of income the tax in respect of *all* your income. Remember, that when the State pension increases, the tax on your other pension or income will go up as the State pension will eat into your tax-free allowance.

At the end of each tax year you should add up your total gross income and tax deducted, to check how much tax you *should* have paid, as detailed in Chapter 12, in case any refund of tax is due to you.

Working after retirement

If you carry on working after the official retirement age (65 or 60) you can still claim the State pension, although you do not have to pay any more National Insurance contributions.

Whether you are employed full time or part time, a PAYE code will be issued (see page 81) that will tax your earnings.

Tax allowances

A husband and wife each have their own tax allowance and are responsible for their own tax affairs.

The tax allowances for 2000–2001 are as follows with the 1999–2000 figures in brackets:

Age by end of tax year	Personal Allowance £	Married Couple's Allowance £
65–74	5,790 (5,720)	5,185 (5,125)
75 and over	6,050 (5,980)	5,255 (5,195)

Tax relief restriction on the married couple's allowance for both years was 10 per cent.

Although the married couple's allowance was abolished from 6 April 2000 it still continues for those couples where either the husband or wife was aged 65 or more on or before 5 April 2000.

The married couple's allowance is based on the age of the *older* of the husband and wife.

These age-related personal allowances, as they are called, are however, reduced if your own total income is above £17,000 (£16,800 for 1999–2000). For every £2 of income above this limit, your allowance is reduced by £1, but no taxpayer can get less than the basic personal allowance (£4,385). Similarly, the married couple's allowance will also be reduced by the excess which has not already been taken into account in calculating the reduced personal allowance. Once again, the allowance cannot be reduced below the minimum level of £2,000 for 2000–2001 (£1,970 for 1999–2000).

Don't forget that a wife's income from all sources is considered separately from that of her husband's.

It is important for married couples to plan their taxable and tax-free income and allocate it beneficially between them in order to avoid what is known as the 'age allowance trap', otherwise some income could effectively be taxed at over 30 per cent.

The following example of a married couple highlights some interesting points. (John, the husband, is aged 74 and his wife, Mary, is 69)

Income for 1999–2000		John's tax £	Mary's tax £
Old age pension, say		3,500	2,050
Other pension, gross amount (tax deducted say £1,380)		7,885	—
Rent from letting unfurnished room (after expenses)		4,046	—
Bank deposit interest – gross amount (received £144 net)		180	—
Dividend – received	£1,800		
– tax credit at 10%	200	2,000	—
National Savings Bank: ordinary interest £40. The first £70 not taxable	40	—	—
Investment account interest		—	50
Total income		17,611	2,100
Less: Personal allowance	£5,720		5,720
Less: Income limit (see note)			(3,620)
(£17,611–£16,800=£811 × 50%)	405		unused
		5,315	allowance
		£12,296	

John's tax liability will be:		£
on his savings income £ 1,500 at 10%		150.00
£ 680 at 20%		136.00
on his other income £10,116 at 23%		2,326.68
		2,612.68
Less: Married couple's allowance		
£5,125 at 10%		512.50
		2,100.18
He has already paid by deduction the following amounts of tax:		
on his other pension	£1,380.00	
on his bank deposit	36.00	
on his dividend	200.00	1,616.00
Tax still to pay		£ 484.18

Notes:

a. John's total income was £17,611; as the income limit is £16,800 his allowances are reduced by £1 for every £2 over this limit. This could have been avoided if some of his income producing assets had been transferred to Mary, his wife.

b. It will be seen that Mary had insufficient income to cover her personal allowance. The unused balance is lost – it cannot be used by her husband. It would have been more sensible for her to have received a greater part of the family income, so they should reconsider reorganising their investments to avoid the same problem arising next year.

How to check your tax for 1999–2000

For the purpose of calculating your total income, you must include the gross amounts of any interest received, including building society and bank interest.

Dividends carry a tax credit in 1999–2000 of 10 per cent of the gross dividend. Basic rate taxpayers have no further tax to pay (see page 86).

If a situation arises where a husband is unable to use part of his married couple's allowance, the balance can be transferred to his wife – ask for Form 575 from your tax office. You have up to five years from the 31 January following the tax year in which to make this request.

If John and Mary, in the above example, were working out their likely tax situation for 2000–2001 they would still get the married couple's allowance as John was over 65 on 6 April 2000 – the amount would be £5,185 at 10 per cent.

The age income limit would be £17,000 and the basic rate of tax would reduce from 23 per cent to 22 per cent.

It will therefore be even more important that John transfers some income bearing investments to his wife, but she should not receive dividends paid net of tax as she cannot reclaim the tax credit; savings paying interest tax free would be preferable (see below).

She should therefore put her savings into tax-free investments or those that pay interest gross without tax being deducted.

Income tax repayment

At the end of each tax year on 5 April you should check to see exactly what income you received during the year and what tax you have actually paid. (See page 84.)

You can get a repayment of tax if you have paid too much.

To reclaim tax ask your tax office for leaflet IR110 and a Form R40. Complete it in the same way as a tax return (see Chapter 4) and send the form to your tax office. There is no need to enclose the dividend and interest vouchers unless the tax office ask for them at a later date.

Where most of your income has already had tax deducted before you receive it (for example interest) you may be able to make quarterly, half-yearly or annual repayment claims (see page 88).

Where to invest your money

In reviewing investments, married pensioners in particular should make sure that they are making full use of both personal allowances.

They should avoid a situation arising where perhaps a husband is paying tax, and his wife is not using her full allowances. To correct such a problem, you should consider switching savings or investments from the husband into his wife's name – she will not pay tax if her total income does not exceed her personal allowance, and the husband's tax will be reduced.

If you have insufficient income to cover your personal allowances it is important to put your savings into investments that pay interest gross, that is, without first deducting tax.

Some suggestions are given below:

Building society and bank accounts

These accounts will pay interest without tax being deducted *provided* you fill in Form R85 and give the completed form to your bank or building society branch. On this form you have to certify that your total income for the tax year is unlikely to exceed your personal allowance. If you are aged 65 to 74 on 6 April 2000 these figures for 2000–2001 are £6,308 for a married man and £5,790 for anyone else; if you are 75 or more they are £6,575 for a married man and £6,050 for anyone else (assuming the husband to be the older married partner).

You will need your National Insurance number to complete this form. If your circumstances change during the tax year and your total income is such that you will become liable to tax you must inform your bank or building society branch immediately.

If you do not complete Form R85, then tax at the lower rate will be deducted from your interest payments and if you are not liable to tax you will have to wait until the following April before claiming any tax back from the tax office. However, if your repayment claim is for £50 or more then you can apply for a refund at any time during the tax year – ask your tax office for leaflet IR110.

National Savings Bonds

Income Bonds are designed for those who wish to receive regular monthly payments of interest while preserving the full cash value of their investment. Interest is paid monthly without tax being deducted, and should be declared on your tax return.

Capital Bonds are similar but interest is added to the capital value annually.

National Savings Bank Accounts

The Investment account gives a higher income than an 'ordinary' account. All interest is liable to tax, except the first £70 on an ordinary account.

Pensioners' Guaranteed Income Bonds

These bonds carry a fixed rate of interest for five years and are specifically for people over 60. Bondholders must have a bank, building society or National Savings investment account to which interest can be transferred automatically. To obtain early repayment 60 days notice is required with a corresponding loss of income.

As with all fixed interest investments you have to be confident that the market interest rates are not going to increase materially over the next few years.

Government Stocks
You can purchase most 'gilt edged' securities at the post office. This will not only save you brokers' fees, but the interest on Government Stocks on the National Savings Stock Register is paid to you regularly without deducting tax. No capital gains tax liability arises on any profit when you sell but the interest should be declared on your tax return.

With all the above investments you should declare the interest in your tax return in the event of your total income (including pensions) exceeding your total allowances, for you will be liable to tax on the difference.

If your income *is* sufficient to cover your allowances then consideration should be given to Building Society and Bank Deposit Accounts, in addition to the above, but also consider:

Index-linked National Savings Certificates
You receive no interest but if held for at least a year your capital is inflation-proofed, and, with annual supplements expanded to 3 per cent compound interest over a five-year period, this 'profit' is exempt from capital gains tax.

Fixed Interest National Savings Certificates
Interest is added throughout the five-year life of the certificate and is free of income tax. You sacrifice some interest if you cash them before the expiry date. The interest does not have to be entered on your tax return.

Bear in mind with the above investments, that you will not get the full benefit of the investment returns if you do not hold the certificates for the full five years.

Chapter 18 on Money Matters gives further investment ideas, including Individual Savings Accounts (ISAs).

Annuities and home income schemes
To improve your standard of living and to increase your spendable income you could mortgage your house to an insurance company and use the lump sum to buy an annuity.

When you receive an annuity payment it consists of two

elements – capital and income. The capital portion is non-taxable but the insurance company will deduct tax from the income portion (which you must enter on your tax return) and provide you with a tax deduction certificate, which you will need to claim any tax repayment. Tax will be deducted at the basic rate of 22 per cent for 2000–2001 (23 per cent for 1999–2000).

You will not get any tax relief on buying the actual annuity. However, provided at least 90 per cent of the lump sum received on mortgaging your house is used to buy the annuity and the loan was taken out before 9 March 1999, then the interest on a mortgage of up to £30,000 will be tax deductible at the basic rate *even though* mortgage interest tax relief is abolished for other loans from 6 April 2000. You must be 65 or over.

It was announced in the March 1999 budget that this relief will be withdrawn for new loans after 9 March 1999 but this will not affect annuity holders nor home income plans taken out before that date.

Annuities are particularly useful if you have no dependants or your children or relatives do not need additional assets.

Bear in mind that any extra income from an annuity could reduce any means-tested social security benefit, could affect your age related personal allowance and will not take inflation into account in succeeding years. Also, you cannot cancel an annuity and get your capital back.

Your pension scheme retirement options

If you are a member of your employer's pension scheme, or have a personal pension scheme of your own, when you retire it is important to consider all of the options.

On your retirement, a tax-free cash lump sum payment is normally available, the calculation of which depends on the type of scheme you hold.

If you are a member of your employer's occupational pension scheme, your lump sum calculation will depend on your years of service and taxable earnings (including P11D benefits) at retirement. You should ask your insurance company or scheme administrator for this information.

If you have your own personal pension plan or retirement annuity, then broadly the tax-free cash lump sum is equivalent to 25 per cent of the total accrued fund available.

The balance of your fund must be used to provide an income which can be paid in one of two ways:

- *either* via an annuity purchased from an insurance company – ask several companies for a quotation taking account of your own circumstances. For instance, do you wish to include a pension for your husband or wife? You should also ask whether your own contract has a guaranteed annuity rate written into the plan since these may be better than those available in the marketplace.

- *or* by drawing down the income from the fund, known as 'Income Drawdown'. This facility is only available up to age 75 to those who hold a personal pension. If, therefore, you are a member of a company scheme or retirement annuity you will need to transfer all the accrued fund before drawing any tax-free cash into a personal pension plan.

Until an annuity is purchased an income can be drawn from the pension fund equivalent to between 35 per cent and 100 per cent of the highest annuity which the fund could have purchased.

This is an extremely complicated area and you should seek specialist independent advice if you wish to investigate these options.

CHAPTER FOURTEEN

Self-employed

A self-employed person is one who owns a business or is in partnership with someone else. If you trade as a limited company, you, as a director, are not self-employed but an employee of that company.

Advantages over PAYE

Self-employed people do not pay PAYE – this method of collecting tax is strictly for employees; instead they pay tax on their profits under what is called 'Schedule D'.

There are definite advantages in paying tax under Schedule D as there are more opportunities for self-employed people to reduce their tax bill than an employed person. There are more expenses that can be claimed and they are somewhat easier to claim. In addition, there is loss relief which can be set against other taxable income or, in the early years of a business, can be carried back against your total income for the previous three years.

If you are self-employed, you may find it more convenient to deal with the paperwork and meet some of your business contacts at your home. This, in effect, becomes a second place of business, so that you can claim against your profits a proportion of the expenses, such as heating and lighting (see page 101).

Start off on the right lines

1. When you start a new business you might have a tax liability in the first year, unless you make a loss or your profit is offset by allowances or reliefs. Do not wait for the tax office to send you a tax return – tell them before 5 October, following your first tax year end of 5 April, that you have started business otherwise you may be penalised.

    You also need to notify the Contributions Agency so that you don't build up arrears of NI contributions or miss out on benefits. The Inland Revenue issue a booklet 'Starting Your Own Business' CWL1 which has useful advice and a form which can be used to notify the relevant departments of your new business.

2. If you do not use your own name you must show the names and addresses of the owners of the business on business letters,

orders, invoices, receipts and demands for payment. You must also display the names and addresses at your business premises.

3. It may be advantageous to take your wife or husband in as a partner if not already employed elsewhere. Do not forget that depending on earnings levels and share of profits, there might be a liability to pay National Insurance contributions (see page 110).

4. When you are in a partnership it is advisable to have a written agreement setting out its terms, particularly if your wife or husband is a partner.

5. You may have been employed before starting up in business on your own. If so, you should send the P45 form you will have received from your previous employer to your local tax office and you may be able to claim a tax refund immediately.

6. You should open a separate bank account for your business which, in the case of a partnership, should be in the partnership names.

7. Keep books detailing your business dealings; the minimum you should keep are a cash book for all monies received and paid, an analysis book for purchases and one for sales, and a petty cash book for miscellaneous expenses.

It is essential that you keep all purchase invoices and copy sales invoices, not only for the purpose of preparing your accounts but also to keep a check on the amounts you may have to pay and charge in respect of value added tax.

Check your turnover to see if you should register for VAT. (See page 139.)

8. Always bear in mind that both the tax inspector and the VAT inspector have a legal right to require you to supply evidence from your books and records for any particular year. You should be especially careful, therefore, not only to have supporting evidence of expenditure which is easily identifiable, but also proof of the accuracy of your income. Under self assessment you must keep books and records for 5 years and 10 months from the end of the tax year.

9. Make regular provision for a retirement pension – see page 130.

10. Check your insurances – advise your insurers if you are operating from your home address or using your own car.

How are you taxed?

Many self-employed people think that you pay tax only on what you take out of the business for yourself as drawings or wages. This is not so.

Drawings are sums taken on account of the profit you expect to make. You are taxed on your total profit before deducting any drawings.

To find out how much profit you have made, you should prepare an account showing your total business income, less your business expenses. This is not necessarily the figure on which your tax is calculated, however, for you have to add any disallowable items mentioned below.

It is this amended profit figure, not the one shown in your accounts, that you should enter in your tax return. Your claim for capital allowances must also be entered (see page 106).

This adjustment and claim for capital allowances is called a 'tax computation'.

Allowable expenses and deductions

Apart from your normal business expenses (e.g. purchase of goods, rent, rates, staff wages) you should consider claiming the following:

1. Hotel and travelling expenses on business trips – not forgetting part of the total running expenses of your car.
2. Part of your private telephone bill.
3. Bank interest and charges on your business account.
4. Business subscriptions and magazines.
5. Special clothing necessary for your type of business, including cleaning costs, etc.
6. Bad and doubtful debts which can be specifically identified.
7. Gifts advertising your business (but the cost must not exceed £10 per person and not be food, drinks, tobacco or vouchers.)
8. Repairs and renewals to business property (e.g. the cost of replacing a shopfront, less any part of that cost representing any improvement).
9. Employer's National Insurance contributions on employee's wages, and on provision of car or fuel benefits (see page 110 for your own NIC deductions).

Expenses and deductions not allowable

It is possible that your business payments include some expenses which are not allowable for tax. In this case, your profit must be increased so as to exclude this private element. Examples of the more usual items are:

A proportion of:

1. Rent, light, heat and council tax – where you live in part of the business premises (e.g. a flat above your shop).

2. Motor car expenses, including hire purchase interest, where you use a business car for private journeys.

3. Telephone bills.

And the whole of:

4. Depreciation on all assets, if included in your accounts, whether they are business or private. You can instead claim capital allowances. (See page 105.)

5. Capital expenditure – the cost of computers, cars, machinery, etc., or expenditure involving improvement as distinct from the repair of an asset. Claim capital allowances instead.

6. Entertaining either UK or foreign customers.

7. Your own earnings.

8. Class 2 and Class 4 NICs. (See page 110.)

9. Donations to political parties.

An example of business accounts and a tax computation is shown below. It has been assumed that Mr Wiltshire has been in business for several years, as there are special rules for new businesses.

An Example of Business Accounts and a Tax Computation

John Wiltshire – Booksellers

Profit and Loss Account for year ended 5 April 2000

	£		£
Opening stock	750	Sales or takings	57,000
Purchases	22,000	Closing stock	2,500
Gross profit	36,750		
	£59,500		£59,500
Staff wages and NIC	6,842	Gross profit	36,750
Rent and rates	4,126	Rent receivable	750
Telephone	427	Profit on sale of	
Light and heat	623	motor car	398
Legal fees re new lease	100		
Carried forward	12,118	Carried forward	37,898

Brought forward	£12,118	Brought forward	£37,898
Insurance of shop	181	Dividends received (after	
Motor expenses	512	tax)	105
Travelling/entertaining	107		
Postage and stationery	87		
General expenses	202		
Bank charges and interest	64		
Depreciation:			
Motor car	600		
Fixtures	376		
Repairs and renewals	789		
Wife's wages	980		
Own wages	10,000		
Own NIC	278		
	26,294		
Net profit	11,709		
	£38,003		£38,003

Although Mr Wiltshire will start with these accounts, various adjustments will have to be made to arrive at an 'adjusted profit for tax purposes'. A 'tax computation' based on the accounts will have to be prepared as follows:

John Wiltshire – Booksellers
PROFIT ADJUSTED FOR INCOME TAX
Year ended 5 April 2000

	£	£
Profit per accounts		11,709
Less: Income taxed separately:		
Rent received	750	
Income on which tax has already been paid:		
Dividends	105	
Profit on sale of motor car	398	
		1,253
		10,456
Add: Items not allowable for tax purposes:		
Own wages and NIC	10,278	
Repairs and renewals – new till	525	
Depreciation: Motor car	600	
Fixtures	376	
General expenses – political donations	22	
Entertaining customers	66	
Motor expenses – 20% private use	102	
Legal fees re new lease	100	
		12,069
Carried forward		22,525

Brought forward			£22,525
Less: Capital allowances		£1,100	
Less: Private use of car	£ 220		
Balancing charge re motor car	144		
		364	
			736
Taxable profit			£21,789

Mr Wiltshire's tax liability is as follows for 1999–2000:

Taxable profit (as above)	£21,789
Deduct: personal pension plan (note 1)	1,820
	19,969
Rent receivable	750
	20,719
Deduct: personal allowance	4,335
Taxable income	£16,384
Total income tax payable £1,500 at 10%	150.00
£14,884 at 23%	3,423.32
	3,573.32
Deduct: Married couple's allowance	
£1,970 at 10%	197.00
	3,376.32
Class 4 NIC payable £21,789 less £7,530 at 6%	855.54
Total tax and NIC payable	£4,231.86

Note 1

Mr Wiltshire paid only £1,820 to a personal pension plan, he could have paid up to £3,813 (17.5% × £21,789) assuming he is under 35 as the maximum allowed (see page 132).

Note 2

If Mrs Wiltshire's wages are going to be her only income next year, she will lose part of her own personal allowance if they stay at their current low level. It would be more tax advantageous to increase her wages to utilise her full allowance and thus reduce the tax paid by Mr Wiltshire on his profits.

Note 3

Mr Wiltshire will make payments on account of his tax and NIC liability on 31 January and 31 July 2000, paying (or receiving) any balance on 31 January 2001.

Simplified accounts

If your turnover is less than £15,000 the self assessment tax return gives you the option of just filling in boxes for your turnover figure, expenses total and net profit, although you will obviously need to compile accounts for your own use to arrive at the figures, and you must keep all documentation in case the tax office have queries at a later date.

Capital allowances

You should set aside part of your profits to save for the replacement of those assets which either become worn out or obsolete. This provision would be shown as depreciation in your accounts,

As mentioned in the previous section, your depreciation provisions are ignored for tax purposes and instead you can claim capital allowances (see table overleaf) as a tax deduction.

Special apportionment rules apply when a business begins or ceases.

Partial claims

If one year's business profit was small enough to be covered by your tax allowances, or you had suffered a trading loss so that you pay no tax, then it would be more worthwhile for you not to claim the whole of the capital allowances; this would keep the written down value for tax purposes higher to give you larger writing down allowances to set against your future profits.

Private use

If you use a business asset for private purposes, for instance, a motor car for weekends and holidays, you must reduce the allowances by the proportion representing your private use.

Buying plant and machinery

It is normally better to buy plant or equipment on the last day of one financial year rather than the first day of your next year – the reason being that you get the equivalent of a full year's capital allowance even though you have owned it for only a matter of hours and, although legally yours, have not necessarily paid for it. You need not pay the whole purchase price, but can buy on hire purchase.

Table of Capital Allowances	First year capital allowance		Writing down % on reducing balance
	Since 1–7–98	From 2–7–97 to 1–7–98	
Plant, machinery and equipment*	40†	50†	25
Fixtures and fittings	40†	50†	25
Motor cars (maximum £3,000 a year)	–	–	25
Vans and lorries	40†	50†	25
Office furniture and equipment	40†	50†	25
Insulation of factories and warehouses	40†	50†	25
Fire safety expenditure	40†	50†	25

For factories and warehouses, agricultural buildings, hotel buildings and houses under assured tenancies schemes there is a writing down allowance of 4 per cent on cost.

† Only applies to small or medium-sized businesses. A new 100 per cent first year allowance was introduced in the March 2000 budget for expenditure on information and communication technology by small businesses in the period 1 April 2000 to 31 March 2003.

* The annual rate of writing down allowance will be reduced to 6 per cent for most assets with a working life of 25 years or more purchased, or contracted, on or after 26 November 1996, but this applies only to businesses which spend more than £100,000 a year on such assets. This 6 per cent is increased to 12 per cent for purchases during the year ended 1 July 1998 by small or medium-sized companies.

Notes: There are higher allowances for buildings in enterprise zones, film production expenditure, and special provisions for patent rights, know how, mines, mineral rights and certain other assets. Research tax credits are available at 150 per cent from 1 April 2000.

The 25 per cent writing down percentage on the reducing balance means effectively that about 90 per cent of the asset is written off after eight years.

The total allowances claimed can never exceed the cost of the asset.

Selling plant and machinery

All plant and machinery with a 25 per cent writing down allowance (other than cars and other assets with an element of private use) is 'pooled' and on any sale you only have to deduct any proceeds of sale before calculating the writing down allowance.

If the proceeds exceed the total value of the pool, after adding the additions for the year, the excess will be charged to tax as a balancing charge. Cars costing up to £12,000 and assets used in part privately, have had to be grouped in separate pools but it was confirmed in the Budget that this unnecessary administrative task can be dispensed with. On cars costing £12,000 or more the maximum allowance is £3,000 a year. Assets used in part privately still have to be grouped in separate pools.

With any other asset acquired on or after 1 April 1986, if you expect to dispose of it within two years for less than the tax written down value, you can elect within two years of the year of acquisition to 'depool' the asset. On disposal, the difference between the tax written down value at that date and the proceeds, if less, will be allowed as an extra relief (known as a balancing allowance), or, if more, charged to tax as a balancing charge.

Your Tax Assessments

For existing businesses

Profits are assessed to tax based on the accounts year ending during the tax year, for example, accounts made up for the year ended 30 June 1999 would be the basis for the 1999–2000 computation; those made up to 5 April 1998 would be for 1997–98.

For new businesses

The date to which you prepare accounts is entirely up to you. Special rules of assessment apply for the first two tax years. For example, if your first accounts are for year ended 30 June 1999, your tax computations will be based as follows:

(a) Year one: 1998–1999   on the profit earned between the 1 July 1998 starting date and 5 April 1999 (apportioned on a time basis).

(b) Year two: 1999–2000   on the profit earned for the first 12 months of trading (i.e. year ended 30 June 1999.)

(c) Year three: 2000–2001   on the accounts for the year ended 30 June 2000.

As you will see in the above example, part of the first year's profits are taxed twice in years one and two (1 July 1998 to 5 April 1999). This is referred to as the overlap profit and details should be kept of the overlapping period and profit as you are able to claim overlap relief if your business ceases or, in certain circumstances, you change the date to which you draw up your accounts.

Your tax bills

You pay tax on your adjusted profit less capital allowances, personal allowances and deductions you will have claimed in your tax return.

Your total tax bill is normally payable by two equal instalments, on 31 January and 31 July in each year, to which is added any Class 4 National Insurance contributions (see page 110).

If you are in a partnership, the partnership profits will still need to be agreed in the firm's name and no partner can independently agree just his own share of the profits. However, the tax liability for each partner will be calculated separately taking into account each partner's personal allowances and reliefs. Partners are no longer responsible for the other partners' tax liabilities. It is best, however, to set aside funds in the partnership to meet each partner's tax liability.

Trading losses

If you should make a loss it can be deducted from:

    (a) other income, and then any capital gains, of the same tax year.

    (b) other income, and then any capital gains, of the previous year.

    (c) trading profits of future years.

    (d) any income in the preceding three tax years, provided the loss arises in the first four tax years of a business, but note that losses are set against the earliest years first.

    (e) any profits over the previous three tax years if the loss arises in the last twelve months before closing down.

Deductions are made in the order that saves most tax.

You cannot claim all your tax reliefs and only a part of the loss; you must claim the whole of the loss first. Therefore before making a claim for loss relief, you should calculate whether you would lose a significant proportion of your personal allowances and deductions.

If, after deducting the loss as suggested above, you find that the remaining income is insufficient to cover your personal allowances, it may be better to carry forward the whole loss with a view to setting it off against future profits from the same trade.

National Insurance contributions

Another liability you have while you are running your own business is National Insurance contributions. Different rules apply to you as a self-employed person – refer to Chapter 14 for details.

Selling up or retiring?

Whether you sell the business, retire, or stop trading for any other reason, you could be faced with revised tax liabilities and possibly capital gains tax.

The problems that might arise on any capital gains liability, and the method of calculation, are dealt with in Chapter 16.

Post cessation receipts

If you receive monies after a business has been discontinued and tax assessments have been finalised, you must declare such income under the *Income* section (Q13) in your tax return; any 'late' relevant expenditure can be offset against such receipts for tax purposes or as a capital loss.

Cash basis assessments

It has been past practice for some professions or vocations to prepare their accounts on the basis of their actual cash receipts, effectively ignoring uninvoiced work-in-progress until completion.

This is being phased out as from 1999–2000 and any amounts which might otherwise escape taxation will be the subject of a one-off catching-up charge over ten years of assessment.

Personal services provided through intermediaries

Although no mention has ever been made of it in any Budget announcements, the Inland Revenue are seeking to treat workers who provide their services via an intermediary such as a service company, and work extensively for one client, as an employee of that client for tax and NIC purposes. This is known as an 'IR35 situation' after the number of the Inland Revenue press release!

The Inland Revenue are concerned at the loss of revenue by virtue of the fact that, for instance, the service company can invoice the client without deducting PAYE or National Insurance contributions and the worker can then take money out of the company in the form of, say, dividends rather than salary, thus avoiding NICs and gaining other tax advantages.

To establish whether you are employed or self-employed for tax purposes will depend on a number of factors, most notably whether an individual invests in his business, risks capital, provides substantial equipment and materials and/or works for a fixed number of hours at another's premises under the direction of a third party – or are you free to come and go as you please and, possibly, have a number of clients.

The new rules take effect from 6 April 2000. Each case will be judged on its merits and the Inland Revenue will give an opinion if asked. Further information is available on their website at www.inlandrevenue.gov.uk or by telephoning 020 7438 7700.

CHAPTER FIFTEEN

National Insurance

Since 1 April 1999 the Contributions Agency has merged with the Inland Revenue so that all enquiries regarding National Insurance contributions, Statutory Sick Pay and Statutory Maternity Pay will be handled by the Inland Revenue.

National Insurance contributions

By law, all employers have to deduct a National Insurance contribution (NIC) from an employee's pay over a certain limit and pass it on to the Government each month or quarter, together with a contribution from the employer.

National Insurance contributions, which are levied on your earnings between certain limits, are not allowed as a deduction from your earnings for tax purposes.

'Earnings' for NIC purposes include bonuses, fees, etc. and any non-business payments made by your employer on your behalf.

There are lower scales of NIC contributions for employees who have contracted out of the State pension scheme and who are members of an approved employer's scheme.

There are six types of National Insurance contribution:

Class 1 – earnings-related contributions payable by most employees, including directors. Employers also have to pay a contribution.

Class 1A – payable by the *employer* on company car benefits and extended to most benefits from 6 April 2000.

Class 1B – payable by employers in respect of PAYE settlement agreements.

Class 2 – a flat rate payable by self-employed persons.

Class 3 – if, for some reason, your contribution record under Classes 1 and 2 is inadequate for you to qualify for some NI benefits you can pay voluntary contributions under this Class to 'make up' your record.

Class 4 – earnings-related contributions payable by self-employed persons and assessed at the same time as income tax. These payments are *in addition* to Class 2 contributions.

A table giving all the rates is reproduced on page 112.

The Inland Revenue NI Contributions Office have a call centre helpline – it is 0645 154627, and for employers ring 0345 143143. If you have complaints about the Inland Revenue NICO write to The Adjudicator's Office, Haymarket House, 28 Haymarket, London, SW1Y 4SP.

NICs on company benefits

Where taxable scale benefits apply to the provision of cars and fuel (see page 51) then any amounts so taxable on the individual are liable to *employer's* national insurance contributions at 12.2 per cent for both 1999–2000 and 2000–2001.

With effect from 6 April 2000 most taxable benefits in kind are liable to employer's national insurance contributions at 12.2 per cent.

This additional NIC liability is payable by the employer annually in arrears in July each year.

Contracting-out

There are lower scales of NIC contributions for employees who have contracted out of the State Earnings Related Pension Scheme (SERPS) and who are members of an approved employer's scheme.

Individuals may also contract out via an appropriate Personal Pension Scheme and have a proportion of both their and their employer's National Insurance contributions, referred to as the contracted-out rebate, paid into their own personal pension plan.

Since 6 April 1998 the rebates are age related and all employees who are, or are considering, contracting out for the first time should review their position with a financial adviser.

Self-employed

All self-employed people are liable to pay flat rate Class 2 NICs either by a direct payment or direct debit through a bank, etc.

If your earnings from self-employment in 2000–2001 are going to be less than £3,825 (1999–2000 £3,770) you should apply at the local tax office to be exempted on the grounds of small earnings.

Inform the Contributions Office if Class 2 contributions are not due for any period (for example, if you are incapacitated). An application for deferral or exemption has to be done annually and *there are strict time limits.*

In addition, you may be liable to pay a Class 4 contribution based on your profits chargeable to tax after deducting any capital allowances.

If, in addition to running your own business, you also have earnings from an employment on which you pay PAYE tax, then you may be liable to pay additional Class 1 National Insurance contributions. However, there is an upper limit on your total liability – ask the Contributions Office for an explanatory booklet.

Statutory sick pay and maternity pay

Employers are responsible for paying statutory sick pay (SSP) to their employees for up to 28 weeks of sickness absence.

SSP is taxable as earnings and the scheme applies to virtually all employees: there are some exceptions, for example those entitled to the State pension, those on low earnings, and certain other categories. The amount you receive depends on your earnings level.

Statutory maternity pay is payable to an employee for a maximum of 18 weeks and can be reclaimed from the Government by the employer.

NATIONAL INSURANCE RATES AND LIMITS

	2000–2001 (1999–2000 in brackets)
CLASS 1 employed earner **STANDARD RATE** for non contracted out employees (see note below)	**Employees** 10% on earnings above £76.01 (£66.00) a week up to and including earnings of £535 (£500) a week. **Employers** 12.2% on earnings above £84.00 (£83.00) a week.
CLASS 1A Company car and fuel benefit	12.2% for employers, based on individual's assessable benefit (see page 51).
CLASS 1B PAYE settlement agreements	12.2% for employers
CLASS 2 Self-employed Small earnings exemption	£2.00 (£6.55) a week £3,825 (£3,770) a year
CLASS 3 Voluntary contributions rate	£6.55 (£6.45) a week
CLASS 4 Self-employed Lower limit of profits or gains Upper limit of profits or gains Maximum contribution	7.0% (6.0%) £4,385 (£7,530) £27,820 (£26,000) £1,640

Note: There are lower percentages for contracted-out employees and reduced rates for certain married women and widows holding a certificate of election (CF383).

CHAPTER SIXTEEN

Capital gains tax

The earlier chapters in this book dealt with tax that may be payable on *income* (that is, your earnings, pensions, investment income, etc.).

You may also be liable to pay tax on gains from *capital* (that is, assets and possessions like land and buildings, shares, antiques, paintings, or a business) when such assets change hands.

The taxation of capital gains has always been complicated and in the 1998 Budget, instead of taking the opportunity to simplify this tax it was made even more complicated by a radical re-organisation.

Therefore, only a concise summary is given here in order to provide background knowledge. If in doubt, seek professional advice.

This chapter deals specifically with disposals by *individuals*. There are special rules for business assets and interests in trusts which are outside the scope of this book.

What is a capital gain?
A capital gain is any profit arising when you sell, transfer, give, receive compensation for, or otherwise dispose of any of your assets or possessions. There is no capital gains tax payable on death but instead you may be liable for inheritance tax. (See Chapter 17).

Is there such a thing as a capital loss?
Yes; obviously it is the reverse of a capital gain, and any capital losses are deducted from any capital gains that you make in the same year. If your capital losses exceed your capital gains, then you cannot claim tax back, but you can carry forward the losses against future gains.

Can you make capital gains without incurring any tax liability?
Yes. There are some specific assets which are free from this tax:

Chattels – such as jewellery, pictures and furniture – where the proceeds are £6,000 or less.

Compensation for damages.

Decorations for gallantry, unless purchased.

Foreign currency for personal use

Gains up to a certain amount on the sale of your business if you are 50 or over, or retiring earlier due to ill health (but see page 119)

Gambling, pools and lottery winnings and prizes

Gifts of outstanding public interest given to the nation

Gifts to charities

Government stocks and public corporation stocks guaranteed by the Government

A house owned and occupied by you which is your main residence – if part let, see page 129, and for claims for use of your home as your office see page 62

Individual savings accounts (ISAs), including the transfer of shares from an employee share scheme

Land and buildings given to the National Trust

Life policies and deferred annuities (unless sold on by original owner)

Mortgage cash-backs from banks and building societies

Motor cars (private)

National Savings Certificates; Premium Bonds

Personal Equity Plan (PEP) investments held for at least a full calendar year, starting 1 January

Qualifying corporate bonds

Save as You Earn schemes

Shares subscribed for under the Business Expansion Scheme (BES) or Enterprise Investment Scheme (EIS)

Shares subscribed for in approved quoted Venture Capital Trusts

TESSA accounts

Annual exemption

You are allowed to make capital gains of £7,200 (1999–2000 £7,100) in each year (after deducting all or part of any capital losses) before you are liable to pay capital gains tax. Most trusts are exempt on the first £3,600 (1999–2000 £3,550).

In addition, there may also be relief for inflation depending on how long you have held an asset. (See page 115.)

Married couples

Each person gets the annual exemption in their own right, and losses cannot be offset between husband and wife.

Transfers of assets made between married couples are treated as taking place for no capital gain or loss. This does not apply if the parties are separated or divorced.

Where an asset has been transferred between married couples, the taper relief (see below) on any later sale or transfer will be based on the combined period of ownership.

Rates of tax

An individual pays capital gains tax on gains above the annual exemption limit at income tax rates as if the gains were added to total income. For 2000–2001 you may therefore pay capital gains tax at the starting rate (10 per cent), savings rate (20 per cent) or higher rate (40 per cent) depending on your other income or a combination of the rates may be used if for example, when added to your other income the gain takes you into the higher rate band.

For 1999–2000 only two tax bands applied – 20 per cent below the basic rate limit or 40 per cent above the basic rate limit (£28,000).

The capital gains of a company are charged to corporation tax, with no annual exemptions, but indexation continues to apply rather than the tapering relief scheme. Trusts have differing rates according to the type of trust and nature of the income.

Can you get relief for inflation?

Yes. In respect of assets held on 5 April 1998 an *indexation allowance* can be claimed for the period of ownership up to 30 April 1998. Thereafter a tapering relief system will be applied to those assets and to assets purchased after 5 April 1998.

(a) **Indexation allowance:** The indexation is based on a value at 31 March 1982 or acquisition value if acquired later, so you will need to know the value at 31 March 1982 for assets acquired before then. Refer to your tax office to obtain the percentage by which the retail prices index has increased either from 31 March 1982 or the date you acquired the asset (if later) to April 1998.

Note that indexation can only be offset against any capital gain – it cannot be used to create or increase a capital loss.

(b) **Tapering relief:** A tapering scale has taken over from indexation since 5 April 1998 (see table on page 116). Assets acquired before 17 March 1998 will qualify for an addition of one year when applying the taper (except for business assets disposed of on or after 6 April 2000).

The taper will be applied to the net gains that are chargeable after the deduction of any current year's losses and losses brought forward from earlier years. The annual exemption amount (see overleaf) will then be deducted from the tapered gains.

CAPITAL GAINS TAPERING RELIEF CHART

GAINS ON BUSINESS ASSETS DISPOSAL ON OR AFTER 6 APRIL 2000			GAINS ON NON-BUSINESS ASSETS		
Number of *complete* years after 5.4.98 for which asset held	Percentage of gain chargeable	Equivalent tax rates for higher rate taxpayer	Number of *complete* years after 5.4.98 for which asset held	Percentage of gain chargeable	Equivalent tax rates for higher rate / basic rate taxpayer (pre-6.4.2000)
		The figure for sales prior to 6.4.2000 are shown in brackets			
0	100 (100)	40 (40)	0	100	40 / 23.00
1	87.5 (92.5)	35 (37)	1	100	40 / 23.00
2	75 (85)	30 (34)	2	100	40 / 23.00
3	50 (77.5)	20 (31)	3	95	38 / 21.85
4	25 (70)	10 (28)	4	90	36 / 20.70
5	25 (62.5)	10 (25)	5	85	34 / 19.55
6	25 (55)	10 (22)	6	80	32 / 18.40
7	25 (47.5)	10 (19)	7	75	30 / 17.25
8	24 (40)	10 (16)	8	70	28 / 16.10
9	25 (32.5)	10 (13)	9	65	26 / 14.95
10 or more	25 (25)	10 (10)	10 or more	60	24 / 13.80

Purchases and sales within a 30 day period are matched so that no gain or loss will be realised for tax purposes so that the practice known as 'bed and breakfasting' has become redundant.

The following example shows how the combination of indexation allowance and taper relief apply:

A non-business asset cost £10,000 in 1989 and is sold or transferred for £20,000 after deducting allowable selling costs, in March 2002.

		£
Disposal proceeds		20,000
Cost	£10,000	
Indexation allowance from 1989 to 1998 based on Inland Revenue index, say	3,000	13,000
Gain before taper relief		7,000
Tapering relief – 4 years taper relief 10% (3 years plus one extra year as asset was held prior to March 1998)		700
Chargeable gain		£6,300

Notes: As the asset was held prior to 17 March 1998 one extra year is added to the number of full years the asset was owned. The taper relief available for business assets is greater.

If the asset had been held prior to 31 March 1982, the value at that date would have been used as the cost, if it was higher than its original cost.

If you elect to rebase the cost of an asset to its 1982 value than *all* chargeable assets have to be valued that way, you cannot be selective.

What is the cost of an asset?

For assets purchased or acquired since 31 March 1982 the initial purchase price (or market value if not purchased), plus expenses incurred before indexation or taper relief is applied will be the cost figure for calculating any capital gain or loss.

For assets held before 31 March 1982 you can use *either* their original cost (or market value if not purchased) plus expenses, *or* the value as at 31 March 1982 whichever gives the smaller gain or loss in each case. Alternatively, you can elect to adopt the 31 March value for all of your assets. Such an election once made and notified to the tax inspector cannot be changed.

How to calculate a capital gain (or loss)

To calculate any capital gains or losses, you need to prepare a schedule showing a brief description of all the assets you have sold; the date and cost of acquisition; value at 31 March 1982 if held at that date; the date of disposal and disposal proceeds.

The next step is to calculate the 'unindexed gain or loss' but at this stage you must decide the figure of cost you are going to adopt. (See above.) You can then work out the gain or loss.

If the result is an unindexed loss this will be the figure you enter in the tax return; if an unindexed gain arises, then refer to the paragraphs on inflation on page 115.

Can you defer paying the tax?

There are two ways in which you can defer paying the tax, either by claiming re-investment relief or roll-over relief.

(a) EIS and VCT deferral: Capital gains tax can be deferred by subscribing for new shares through the enterprise investment scheme (EIS) or new shares in approved quoted venture capital trusts (VCT); in such cases the capital gains tax deferral is in addition to the 20 per cent income tax relief.

(b) Roll-over relief: Capital gains tax on a gain from the sale of a business asset can be deferred by re-investing the proceeds in other business assets. If a business is sold as a going concern to a company in exchange for its shares, capital gains tax on the gain can be deferred.

What to enter in your 2000 tax return

Remembering that the 2000 tax return will apply to capital gains for the year ending 5 April 2000, if your chargeable gains do not exceed £7,100 *and/or* the total proceeds of sale do not exceed £14,200, there is no need to make any entry at all in this part of your tax return. However, it is wise to keep all your schedules and workings, for it is possible that at a later date you, or the tax office, may wish to refer to them. You may also want to complete the capital gains pages of your tax return to claim a capital loss.

As mentioned at the beginning of this chapter, the capital gains tax legislation can be very complicated – only a brief outline has been given here. There are, for example, complex rules for valuing assets held before the introduction of this tax in 1965; there are 'pooling' provisions for identical shares acquired on different dates; there are special rules for business assets.

Inherited assets (chargeable assets acquired)

Contrary to many people's belief *you do not generally* have to pay capital gains tax on receiving cash or assets left to you under a will or settlement. Assets only become liable (subject to the normal exemption rules) when you dispose of them.

Paying capital gains tax

Since 1996–97 capital gains tax has been payable with any balance of income tax due on the following 31 January each year.

Self-employed: retirement relief

If you are aged 50 or over when you sell or transfer the whole or part of a business (including a partnership), or shares in a family trading company or group of which you were a full-time working director, up to £250,000 of any capital gain on disposals may be tax-free. In addition, there is a 50 per cent relief on any gains between £250,000 and £1 million.

Gains on assets you own personally but allow your trading partnership or company to use rent free can also attract the 'retirement relief' provided the sale of the assets is linked to a withdrawal or partial withdrawal from the business activities.

If you have to retire before your 50th birthday due solely to ill health, then you can still qualify for the relief.

In order to take advantage of the full relief you must have been in business continuously for ten years up to the sale or transfer. However, an appropriate percentage of the relief is given so long as you have owned the business or shares for at least one year.

Note, however, that this retirement relief is being phased out as from 6 April 1999 by reducing the exemption levels over a five year period as follows:

*Year	100% relief on gains up to:	50% relief on gains between:
1998–99	£250,000	£250,001–£1,000,000
1999–00	£200,000	£200,001–£800,000
2000–01	£150,000	£150,001–£600,000
2001–02	£100,000	£100,001–£400,000
2002–03	£50,000	£50,001–£200,000

*During this period taper relief will be available on any gains which remain chargeable after allocation of retirement relief.

CHAPTER SEVENTEEN

Inheritance tax

M ost of the chapters in this book have dealt with tax payable on your *income*. Chapter 16 dealt with tax payable on *capital items* (capital gains tax) when such assets change hands *during* your lifetime.

Having paid all such liabilities, you are still not free of the tax inspector, for inheritance tax may have to be considered. Inheritance tax may be payable not only on the value of your estate on death, but also on lifetime gifts.

Most taxes have complex rules and provisions, mainly to avoid fraud, and this tax is certainly no exception. In this book it is only possible to deal broadly with the main provisions and exemptions. You should consult an accountant or solicitor if you need specific planning advice, or you have to deal with someone else's estate.

Inheritance tax payable on death

When you die, the tax inspector regards you as having made a 'transfer' of your estate and it will be valued accordingly.

Certain legacies are allowed as a deduction from the value, however:

(a) Legacies for the benefit of the nation or for the public benefit, including funds to maintain historic property.

(b) Legacies between husband and wife provided both are domiciled in the UK.

(c) Legacies to a charity.

(d) Legacies to political parties.

(e) Legacies of certain heritage property and woodlands.

In addition, the value of any lifetime gifts which were either chargeable lifetime gifts or gifts that have become chargeable because death has occurred within seven years will be added to the value of your estate on death. (These gifts are *valued at the time they were made* rather than the value at the date of death.)

Inheritance tax payable on lifetime gifts

There are three types of lifetime gift: specifically exempt gifts, gifts that *may* be exempt and chargeable lifetime gifts.

1. Specifically exempt gifts

The following are gifts which are exempt:

(a) All gifts between a husband and wife, provided both are domiciled in the UK.

(b) Gifts up to a total of £3,000 in any one year plus any unused amount of the previous year's exemption. (You can carry over unused relief for a maximum of one year.)

(c) In addition to the £3,000 referred to above, individual gifts not exceeding £250 to different persons in any one tax year are exempt.

(d) Additional gifts may be exempt if a person makes them as part of normal expenditure made out of income.

(e) Gifts arranged beforehand in consideration of marriage as follows:

Giver	Gift limit
Bridegroom to bride, or vice versa	£2,500
Parents of either	£5,000
Grandparents or remoter ancestors of either	£2,500
Any other person	£1,000

(f) All gifts to political parties, or UK established charities.

(g) Lump sums received from a pension scheme on death or retirement if used to purchase a pension for yourself or dependants.

(h) Gifts for the benefit of the nation or public, e.g. universities, the National Trust.

(i) Maintenance payments to ex-husbands or wives.

(j) Reasonable gifts to support a dependant relative.

(k) Gifts for the education and maintenance of your children, if under 18.

2. Gifts that may be exempt

Gifts to individuals (other than those in the exempt list above), gifts into accumulation and maintenance trusts, and gifts into trust for the disabled are also exempt from inheritance tax provided they are not made within seven years of death. These are called potentially exempt transfers.

If inheritance tax is payable due to the death occuring within seven years, there is a tapering relief from the full tax rate.

It can therefore sometimes happen that if you receive a gift and the person giving the gift dies, you may have to pay the inheritance tax on that gift at a later date.

3. Chargeable liftime gifts

Generally speaking, these are all other gifts not covered in 1 and 2 above and inheritance tax is payable to the tax inspector at the time a gift is made, once the total value of such gifts made within any seven year period goes above the nil tax band. In these cases the tax rate payable is one half of the full inheritance tax rate.

Rates of inheritance tax

From 6 April 2000			From 6 April 1999	
Tax rate %	Chargeable transfer		Tax rate %	Chargeable transfer
	£			£
Nil	£234,000		Nil	£231,000
40	Over £234,000		40	Over £231,000

Tapering Relief

Years between gift and death:	0–3	3–4	4–5	5–6	6–7
% of full charge at death rates:	100%	80%	60%	40%	20%

There are special valuation rules and reduced rates of tax for business property and agricultural property, certain gifts to preservation trusts, historic houses and works of art.

Who pays the inheritance tax?

It is the responsibility of the executors of a Will to pay any taxes due before distributing the assets to the beneficiaries, but in respect of gifts made within seven years of death the executors could ask the person who received the gift to bear any inheritance tax that may apply to it, unless there was a clause in the Will specifically authorising the estate to bear all the taxes arising.

Quick succession relief

The legislation covering the inheritance tax where the same assets become liable to tax due to deaths arising within five years of one another is very complicated, but broadly there is relief on a tapering scale.

Small businesses

Over the past few years most Budgets have extended reliefs to reduce the impact of inheritance tax on the transfer of interests in small business and agricultural concerns.

In respect of sales or disposals on or after 10 March 1992, inheritance tax was abolished on interests in unincorporated businesses; holdings above 25 per cent in unlisted and USM companies (relief was 50 per cent prior to 6 April 1996); owner-occupied farmlands and farm tenancies. There is a 50 per cent relief for controlling holdings in quoted companies and on certain business assets owned by partnerships and interests in possession.

The rules, regulations and conditions, both as regards type of business and period of ownership prior to death are numerous and complex.

It is important to consult professional advisers when considering such matters.

Wills

You should always make a will regardless of how much you own. This will prevent your dependants being unduly troubled and will mean that your wishes will be carried out legally and properly.

Although there are do-it-yourself Will packages available, it does not cost a lot to go through a solicitor, and you will then have expert, experienced advice on which to draw.

If you don't leave a valid Will you will be regarded as having died intestate and your assets will be distributed under strict legal rules, which certainly may not be what you intended.

If you are not sure what to do with your estate, then you can set up a discretionary trust in your Will, appoint trustees, and they will have two years in which to give away your assets; you will doubtless have discussed your general intentions with your selected trustees during your lifetime, so that they have a good idea of your wishes.

CHAPTER EIGHTEEN

Money matters

A s well as taking care of your family tax affairs it is a good idea to know some of the best kinds of financial planning available, not only for the present but also for the future.

If you are married refer to Chapter 10 to ensure that you have allocated investments between husband and wife to make the best use of the tax system.

Here is a general summary of the various forms of savings and investment opportunities that might be considered:

Building Society Deposit or Share Accounts – these combine safety with easy access and a flexible rate of interest. They are particularly useful if you are saving for eventual house purchase as building societies tend to give preference to existing investors.

Interest is paid after having the tax deducted at the savings rate of 20 per cent. If your total income is unlikely to exceed your personal allowance you can fill in Form R85, and once the building society receive this completed form they will pay interest gross.

Bank Deposit Accounts – banks are now more flexible in the variety of deposit accounts and interest you can have to suit your particular needs. The interest has tax deducted at the savings rate of 20 per cent, but non-taxpayers can receive payments gross by filling in the appropriate form (see Building Society Accounts above).

National Savings Bank – like the building society account, this is an easy method of saving, and it is easily withdrawn. Only the National Savings Bank ordinary interest is partially tax-free (see page 12) depending on the total amount in the account. The investment account interest is paid gross, but is still taxable.

National Savings Certificates – the fixed rate of interest is tax free and is added annually to your capital at an increasing rate over a period of five years. The certificates can quite easily be withdrawn during the five years but you will lose a part of the total interest. Note also Index Linked National Savings Certificates, the interest on which is based on the increase in the retail prices index, plus three per cent per year compound interest guaranteed over five years.

Pensioners Guaranteed Income Bonds – these are detailed on page 95.

National Savings Income and Capital Bonds – should also be considered (see page 95).

Children's Bonus Bonds – a high interest savings scheme for children under the age of 16. The Bonds can be purchased at any post office. On each anniversary interest is added plus, on the fifth anniversary (up to the age of 21), a bonus. Both interest and bonus are tax-free.

Tax-Exempt Special Savings Account – anyone over 18 could open a TESSA account with a bank or building society until 5 April 1999 after which no new TESSA accounts could be started. A maximum of £9,000 could be deposited over a five year period.

The interest is free of tax for the first five years provided that no capital is withdrawn. All tax advantages are lost if there are any capital withdrawals.

There *is* a facility for the interest only to be withdrawn, but in that event an amount equal to the basic rate tax will be deducted.

It is important to remember that the rate of interest is not guaranteed throughout the five years (as it is, for example, with National Savings Certificates) and the interest could go down if interest rates decline generally.

Prior to 5 April 1999, if your first TESSA had matured, some or all of the capital could be put into a second TESSA opened within six months of the maturity of the first TESSA. If this amount was less than £9,000, up to £1,800 a year could be added, up to the £9,000 overall limit.

TESSAs were replaced with a new tax-free **Individual Savings Account** (ISA) from 6 April 1999 – see page 126.

Personal Equity Plans (PEP) – under such plans if you were 18 or over and resident in the UK you could invest up to a maximum of £6,000 each tax year in quoted shares or qualifying unit trusts, corporate bonds, investment trusts, preference and convertible shares. The limits could be exceeded to take up rights issues provided that the shares were purchased before the announcement of the issue. However, no new investments could be made in PEPs after 5 April 1999.

In addition to the above limits a person could invest up to £3,000 in a single-company PEP.

The tax benefits of a PEP were that any dividends received, and reinvested interest would be free from tax, and any capital gains would be free of capital gains tax.

All-employee share schemes could also be transferred to a single-company PEP without incurring capital gains tax.

PEPs have been replaced with a new tax free Individual Savings Account (ISA) from 6 April 1999.

Individual Savings Account (ISA) – this new-tax free savings account started on 6 April 1999 and will run for a minimum of 10 years.

All UK residents over the age of 18 can open such an account *regardless* of the value of any existing PEPs or TESSAs.

All income and capital gains arising from the account will be free of tax and the Government will additionally provide a ten per cent tax credit each year for the first five years on dividends from UK equities.

The maximum investment in the first and second years will be £7,000 of which not more than £3,000 must be in cash (e.g. National Savings, bank deposits) and not more than £1,000 in life insurance. In both instances you can invest up to the annual maximum wholly in stocks and shares.After the first two years, the limit will be £5,000 with not more than £1,000 in cash and £1,000 in life insurance.

Husbands and wives each have their own limit.

There will be no penalty for withdrawals at any time, except that if you subscribe the maximum amount in a year and then withdraw sums, you will not be allowed to replenish the account until the start of the next tax year.

There are two types of ISA – maxi and mini!

Under a maxi ISA savers can spread their money between cash deposits, shares and insurance in a single plan run by one financial company. With a mini ISA savers may use one financial service provider for shares, another for cash and a third for insurance – BUT cannot have a mix of mini and maxi ISAs being started in the same year. If you want to make the maximum investment in stocks and shares you will need to have a maxi ISA. It's all so unnecessarily complicated!

Unit Trusts – these are a way for the small investor to benefit from investing in a wide range of companies. Many trusts nowadays specialise in different areas of investment – some with emphasis on capital growth, or income, or overseas companies, etc. You can purchase units directly from the unit trust company, or through a bank or broker. You pay tax on the income and gains in the normal way. (Many personal equity plans offer unit trust investment.)

Finance Houses – these are businesses which generally pay a higher rate of interest than the average market rate. It is important to consult an accountant or solicitor to obtain an opinion as to a particular finance house's financial stability.

Permanent Interest Bearing Shares (PIBs) – these are building society shares which are listed on the stock exchange and are traded on the stock market. There is a fixed rate of interest. They are not as secure as gilt edged investments, or building society accounts, and they are not as marketable when you wish to sell.

Bonds – the Bond market is expanding rapidly with many variations such as investment bonds, guaranteed income bonds, fixed rate bonds, etc.

They are all a method of investing a lump sum with a variable or fixed rate of interest with returns varying according to the type of investment in which the bond company specialises. Watch carefully for hidden charges that could eat into your capital and bear in mind that you could lose if interest rates rise and you are locked into a fixed rate over a number of years, for it is often expensive to negotiate premature repayment.

Government stocks – these stocks, known as gilt edged securities, are quoted on the stock exchange. They can be purchased through a bank, broker or your local Post Office.

Since 6 April 1998 new holders of all types of Government Stocks will receive the interest gross. This is beneficial and will delay the payment of any tax, but don't forget that you may have to pay over this tax after the tax year finishes. (If you *want* to have tax deducted from your interest you *can* elect to do so when you buy the shares.) Profits on sale are free from capital gains tax.

Ordinary shares in quoted companies – buying shares quoted on the stock exchange is a gamble, for the share price of even the most well-known names can fluctuate considerably over a short period. You should obtain professional advice before investing.

Dividends are paid after allowing for a tax credit. This was 20 per cent prior to 5 April 1999, but has been reduced to 10 per cent from that date.

If you are a non-taxpayer you were able to claim this back up to 5 April 1999 but after that date it cannot be reclaimed and it may be more beneficial to put savings into investments that pay gross interest without any tax deductions (see pages 94 and 124).

The amount of dividend received, plus the tax credit, has to be added to your total income in working out your overall tax liability and if this takes you into the higher rate band, then more tax will be payable. If you are a basic rate taxpayer, there is no further liability.

Enterprise Investment Scheme (EIS) – Under these schemes, an individual can gain tax relief on investments in unquoted trading companies. The main provisions are:

(a) income tax relief is given at 20 per cent on qualifying investments up to £150,000 in any tax year;

(b) gains on disposal are exempt from capital gains tax;

(c) there is income tax or capital gains tax relief for losses on disposal;

(d) eligible shares must be held for at least five years (reduced to three years for shares issued on or after 6 April 2000);

(e) relief on up to one-half of the amount an individual invests between 6 April and 5 October in any year can be carried back to the previous tax year, subject to a maximum of £25,000.

(f) A chargeable gain can be reinvested in an EIS to obtain a deferral of capital gains tax.

(g) For eligible shares issued on or after 6 April 1998 the subscription must be wholly in cash.

The rules and regulations governing Enterprise Investment Schemes are very complex. Do seek professional advice before investing.

Venture Capital Trusts were introduced in 1995 to encourage individuals to invest indirectly in unquoted trading companies.
The main provisions are:

(a) individuals are exempt from tax on dividends and capital gains tax arising from shares acquired, up to £100,000 a year, in these trusts.

(b) income tax relief of 20 per cent on up to £100,000 in any tax year for subscribing for new shares held for at least five years (reduced to three years for shares issued on or after 6 April 2000).

Investing in property – Investing in a second property may provide a safe investment over a longer period, even though any profit you might make on selling would be subject to capital gains tax. For tax relief on interest on borrowing for such a purpose, see page 68 and for the tax treatment of property income and Rent-a-Room schemes see page 63.

Your house and mortgage

Your family home: The three most common ways of financing house purchase are by a loan from a building society, a local council or through one of the major banks or financial institutions. However, in order to add a savings element in the general financing package consider a **pension mortgage**.

This is similar to an endowment mortgage, but the advantage is that it is very tax efficient, for although you do not get tax relief on the interest element since 6 April 2000, the payments into the pension plan are fully tax deductible at your top tax rate.

Up until 5 April 1999 it was also possible to use a personal equity plan (PEP) to fund a mortgage by taking out an interest-only mortgage plus a life policy and using the PEP for capital repayments. You could use several PEPs, not just one. Mortgages linked to ISA policies are now available instead.

Selling your house – Any profit you make on selling the property you own and live in is free from capital gains tax. Where you own two houses at the same time as a result of not being able to sell the first, no capital gains tax will arise on either house, provided you sell the first house within three years.

Even if you let part of your own house, you are unlikely to pay tax on the proportion of the profit you make when you sell because the gain in respect of the let portion will be tax free if it is not more than the private residence proportion up to a maximum of £40,000.

Should you pay off the mortgage early? – A mortgage loan is the cheapest way to borrow money with interest rates far lower than personal loans and credit cards even though the tax relief on the interest has now been abolished.

Therefore you must decide whether you can achieve a better return after tax on your investment, bearing in mind that there is no such thing as a low risk, high return investment. Also check whether there is a charge by the lender for paying off the mortgage early. You must also consider your likely cash needs in future years.

Charitable giving

Payroll giving schemes – Employers are allowed to run these schemes under which an employee can make donations to charity.

The donation is deducted from your pay, and passed on to the charity by your employer. PAYE is calculated on your salary *after* making the deduction so that you are effectively getting immediate tax relief on the donation at your highest tax rate. A husband and wife who both pay tax under PAYE can each give the maximum donation and get tax relief. The maximum was £1,200 a year until 5 April 2000 but there is now no limit.

Gift aid – This scheme applies to single gifts made by individuals and charities. Further details are given on page 71.

Covenants – A deed of covenant is a legally binding agreement and is a longer term commitment to giving to a charity. It has to be for a period exceeding three years to get tax relief.

You get this relief by deducting tax at the basic rate from the payment. If you are a higher rate taxpayer any excess can be claimed on your tax return.

It is important to note, however, that you can only benefit from this tax relief if you are a taxpayer yourself. If your income does not cover your personal allowances then you will have to pay back the tax deducted to the tax inspector.

Pension options:
Pension schemes – In general, contributing to a pension scheme is a good idea because:

(a) The tax inspector will pay part towards your pension as the contributions are allowable for tax at your top rate.

(b) The pension scheme will provide you with additional income to supplement your State pension when you retire.

(c) A tax free capital sum can be taken on retirement.

There are now four ways in which you can contribute to a pension scheme:

(i)   An **employer's scheme,** whereby either your employer, or both of you, contribute to the scheme. Any contribution you make will be deducted from your salary before PAYE is calculated, and this is how you will get your tax relief. The maximum total payment for tax relief is 15 per cent of your earnings (including benefits in kind). Remember that the 15 per cent relief *includes* any contributions you are contractually required to make to your employer's scheme. Many employers offer pension provision via a *group* personal pension scheme where the maximum contribution will be higher since they are age related (see page 132).

(ii) **Additional Voluntary Contributions** (AVCs) – these are top up payments over and above the contribution being paid to your main employer's scheme and are also deducted from your salary before PAYE is calculated. These schemes normally offer good value. You do not have to take the benefit at the same time as your main pension, but at any time from 50 to 75 years of age.

(iii) **Free-Standing Additional Voluntary Contributions** (FSAVC) – instead of topping up extra sums to your employer's scheme, you can pay into a separate scheme and deduct tax at the basic rate before paying the premiums. If you are a higher rate taxpayer, any additional relief would be claimed on your tax return and is normally reflected by an adjustment to your PAYE coding allowance. Again the 15 per cent overall limit applies.

(iv) **Personal pension plans.** If you are self-employed, or not a member of an employer's pension scheme, you can get tax relief on the payments made to a personal pension plan. As mentioned on the previous page your employer may be operating a group personal pension scheme instead of an occupational pension scheme for all their employees. You can have more than one personal pension plan. The total maximum available for tax relief as a percentage of earnings (or profits if you are self-employed) is shown below.

You obtain tax relief for retirement annuity premiums on policies taken out before 1 July 1988 by claiming on your tax return. For personal pension plans after that date, if you are employed, tax is deducted from the premium at the basic rate – any higher rate tax relief is claimed on your tax return. The self-employed also claim on their tax return.

If, during the last six years, you have not been able to contribute the maximum premiums allowed for full tax relief (and you cannot include years when you were in pensionable employement), you are allowed to get extra tax relief by making use of any unused 'balance' – this is known as 'carry forward relief'. (This can only be done if you have first contributed the maximum in the current year.)

When paying the contribution you will need to complete form PP42 and send it to your tax office. This procedure is to end with the introduction of stakeholder pensions (see below).

You are also able to pay a contribution during the 2000–2001 tax year and carry the payments back one year to the 1999–2000 tax year and have it offset against your income in that year. With the introduction of stakeholder pensions you will only be able to carry back contributions paid by 31 January in the following tax year.

This is particularly attractive to those whose incomes vary and especially if in the current year you will only be a basic rate taxpayer but in the 1999–2000 tax year you paid higher rate tax. Form PP43 should be completed and sent to your tax office.

Refer to page 96 for further details on the purchase of annuities.

Age at beginning of tax year	Retirement annuity premium	Personal pension plan
	%	%
up to 35	17.5	17.5
36 to 45	17.5	20
46 to 50	17.5	25
51 to 55	20	30
56 to 60	22.5	35
61 and over	27.5	40

For plans taken out after 14 March 1989 the maximum net relevant earnings figures on which relief is available are as follows:

From 6 April:	1991	£71,400	1994	£76,800	1997	£84,000
	1992	£75,000	1995	£78,600	1998	£87,600
	1993	£75,000	1996	£82,200	1999	£90,600

The figure from 6 April 2000 will be £91,800.

From 6 April 2001, personal pension plans will be replaced by stakeholder pensions. Contributions of up to £3,600 will be allowable without reference to earnings, thereafter, higher contributions will be based on age and a percentage of earnings. This will extend the opportunity to have a pension to many people who were unable to make such investments previously as they had no earnings, e.g. housewives.

Self assessment –
Tax calculation working sheets

If you want to calculate your tax when you send in your tax return, you need to tick the appropriate 'Yes' box in Q18 on page 7 of your tax return.

You will need to fill in the Tax Calculation Guide provided by your tax office with your tax return (telephone 0845 9000 404 if you haven't been sent one and you want a guide).

All the boxes are numbered according to the boxes in the main tax return and any supplementary pages that you need to complete, and although these forms look very complicated it is really a question of transferring all the figures into the correct summary boxes and following the instructions to ensure that you do the additions and subtractions according to the sequence.

Only the summary pages of the tax calculation working sheets are reproduced here. The sheets have been revised this year and now run to 27 pages.

To complicate matters, you will need a different set of sheets if you have chargeable gains, or have received compensation payments, or AVC refunds, but these are mentioned specifically in the tax notes that come with your tax return.

Even if you don't use these pages to calculate your own tax, you can use them to understand, and check, the tax office statement when it is sent to you.

Tax Calculation Working Sheet

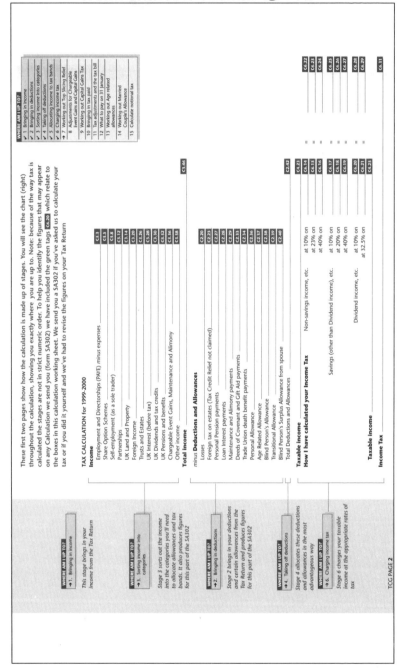

WHERE AM I UP TO?

1 Bringing in income
2 Bringing in deductions
3 Sorting income into categories
4 Taking off deductions
5 Allocating income to tax bands
6 Charging income tax
7 Working out Top Slicing Relief
8 Adjustments for Chargeable Event Gains and Capital Gains
9 Working out Capital Gains Tax
10 Bringing in tax paid
11 Tax adjustments and the tax bill
12 What to pay on 31 January
13 Working out Age related allowances
14 Working out Married Couple's Allowance
15 Calculate notional tax

These first two pages show how the calculation is made up of stages. You will see the chart (right) throughout the calculation, showing you exactly where you are up to. Note: because of the way tax is calculated the stages are not in strict numeric order. To help you identify the figures that may appear on any Calculation we send you (form SA302) we have included the green tags C3.20 which relate to the boxes in this calculation working sheet. We send you a SA302 if you've asked us to calculate your tax or if you did it yourself and we've had to revise the figures on your Tax Return

TAX CALCULATION for 1999-2000

Income

Employment and Directorships (PAYE) *minus expenses*	C3.3
Share Option Schemes	C3.5
Self-employment (as a sole trader)	C3.8
Partnerships	C3.12
UK Land and Property	C3.14
Foreign Income	C3.20
Trusts and Estates	C3.26
UK Interest (before tax)	C3.28
UK Dividends and tax credits	C3.30
UK Pensions and benefits	C3.32
Chargeable Event Gains, Maintenance and Alimony	C3.36
Other income	C3.38
Total Income	**C3.46**

minus Deductions and Allowances

Losses	C2.20
Foreign tax on estates (Tax Credit Relief not claimed)	C2.23
Personal Pension payments	C2.27
Loan Interest payments	C2.28
Maintenance and Alimony payments	C2.29
Deeds of Covenant and Gift Aid payments	C2.31
Trade Union death benefit payments	C2.34
Personal Allowance	C2.36
Age Related Allowance	C2.37
Blind Person's Allowance	C2.38
Transitional Allowance	C2.39
Blind Person's Surplus Allowance from spouse	C2.40
Total Deductions and Allowances	**C2.42**

Taxable Income

How I have calculated your Income Tax

Non-savings income, etc.	at 10% on	C4.23
	at 23% on	C4.14
	at 40% on	C4.15
		C4.16
Savings (other than Dividend income), etc.	at 10% on	C4.17
	at 20% on	C4.18
	at 40% on	C4.19
Dividend income, etc.	at 10% on	C4.20
	at 32.5% on	C4.21
		C4.23

Taxable Income

Income Tax

This stage brings in your income from the Tax Return

WHERE AM I UP TO?
→ 1. Bringing in income

WHERE AM I UP TO?
→ 3. Sorting income into categories

Stage 3 sorts out the income into the categories you'll need to allocate allowances and tax bands. It also produces figures for this part of the SA302

WHERE AM I UP TO?
→ 2. Bringing in deductions

Stage 2 brings in your deductions and certain allowances from the Tax Return and produces figures for this part of the SA302

WHERE AM I UP TO?
→ 4. Taking off deductions

Stage 4 allocates these deductions and allowances in the most advantageous way

WHERE AM I UP TO?
→ 6. Charging income tax

Stage 6 charges your taxable income at the appropriate rates of tax

TCC PAGE 2

Tax Calculation Working Sheet

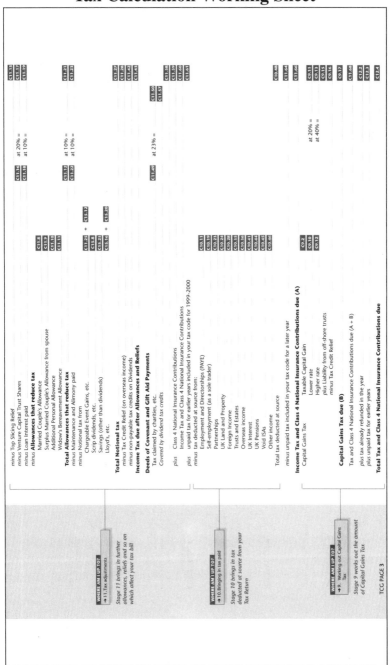

WHERE AM I UP TO?
→ 11. Tax adjustments

Stage 11 brings in further
allowances, reliefs and so on
which affect your tax bill

WHERE AM I UP TO?
→ 10. Bringing in tax paid

Stage 10 brings in tax
deducted at source from your
Tax Return

WHERE AM I UP TO?
→ 9. Working out Capital Gains
Tax

Stage 9 works out the amount
of Capital Gains Tax

TCG PAGE 3

Working sheets

The way in which the self assessment tax return is designed means that you can only put one figure in each box. Therefore, if, for example, you have dividends from six companies, you need to add them together and put the total figure in your tax return; it is essential to keep a record of how you arrived at this figure, therefore the following grids are provided for you to use as working sheets for various sources of income or expenditure.

Q10	Dividends			
Box Number		10.2	10.3	10.4
		Net	Tax Credit	Gross
	Totals £	£	£	

Employment Supplementary Sheet
Expenses claimed Boxes 1.32 to 1.36
Detail   £
Total   £

Working Sheets

Q13	Other income			
	Box Number	13.1	13.2	13.3
		Net	Tax deducted	Amount before tax
	Totals	£	£	£

Losses

		£
	Totals	£

		£
	Totals	£

Personal reminders

National Insurance Number . . . .

Tax Reference Number . . . .

Tax Office Address . . . .

. . . .

. . . .

Tax Returns	*Date sent to tax office*	*Date agreed with Inland Revenue*
1998–99	. . . .	. . . .
1999–2000	. . . .	. . . .
2000–2001	. . . .	. . . .

	1999–2000	2000–2001	2001–2002
PAYE Code checked	☐	☐	☐
P60 Form from employer checked	☐	☐	☐
P11D Form checked	☐	☐	☐

Notes on correspondence:

. . . .

. . . .

. . . .

. . . .

. . . .

Rates of tax and allowances

Income tax	2000–2001	1999–2000	1998–1999
Starting rate at 10%	£1,520	£1,500	—
Lower rate at 20%	—	—	£4,300
Basic rate at 22%	£1,521–£28,400	—	—
Basic rate at 23%	—	£1,501–£28,000	£4,301–£27,100
Higher rate at 40%	over £28,400	over £28,000	over £27,100

Income tax is payable on your total income, earned and unearned after deducting your personal allowances and allowable expenses.

The lower rate at **20 per cent** applies to **savings income** for basic rate taxpayers but for 1999–2000 and 2000–2001 savings income (other than dividends) can be allocated to the starting rate band at 10%. See page 87 for dividend tax rates.

Capital gains tax
The rate for individuals is the same as their individual tax rate.

Exemption limit	£7,200	£7,100	£6,800

Inheritance tax
Rate 40% –

Exemption limit	£234,000	£231,000	£223,000

VAT rate	*17½%	*17½%	*17½%
VAT registration turnover level	£52,000 from 1.4.2000	£51,000 from 1.4.99	£50,000 from 1.4.98
VAT deregistration turnover level	£50,000 from 1.4.2000	£49,000 from 1.4.99	£48,000 from 1.4.98

*5% on domestic fuel (8% prior to 1.9.97)

Corporation tax – The rate for 1999–2000 through to 2001–2002 is 30% and 20% for small companies. For companies with trading profits up to £10,000 the rate is 10% from 1.4.2000 with marginal relief up to £50,000.

Personal allowance	£4,385	£4,335	£4,195
Married couple's **allowance**	Nil	††£1,970	†£1,900
Age allowance			
Aged 65–74 personal	£5,790	£5,720	£5,410
married couple's	††£5,185	††£5,125	†£3,305
Aged 75 personal	£6,050	£5,980	£5,600
& over married couple's	††£5,255	††£5,195	†£3,345
Minimum amount	††£2,000	††£1,970	†£1,900
but there are income restrictions.			
Income limit	£17,000	£16,800	£16,200
Additional personal **allowance**	Nil	††£1,970	†£1,900
Widow's bereavement	Nil	††£1,970	†£1,900
Blind person's **allowance**	£1,400	£1,380	£1,330

† relief restricted to 15 per cent.   †† relief restricted to 10 per cent.

Summary of Working Families' and Disabled Person's tax credits

Working Families' Tax Credit		
	1999–2000	**2000–2001**
	£	£
Basic credit	52.30	53.15
30 hours credit	11.05	11.25
Child credits		
Under 11	19.85	*21.25
11–16	20.90	*21.25
16–18	25.95	26.35
Disabled child – from October 2000	—	22.25
Income threshold	90.00	91.45
*Increased to £25.60 from June 2000		

Disabled Person's Tax Credit		
	1999–2000	**2000–2001**
	£	£
Basic credit – single	54.30	55.15
– lone parent/couples	83.55	84.90
30 hours credit	11.05	11.25
Child credits		
Under 11	19.85	*21.25
11–16	20.90	*21.25
16–18	25.95	26.35
Disabled child	21.90	22.25
Income threshold – single	70.00	71.10
– lone parent/couple	90.00	91.45
*Increased to £25.60 from June 2000		

Note: The 11–16 and 16–18 child credits are paid from the September following the 11th birthday and 16th birthday respectively.

Social Security Benefits
Rates weekly unless otherwise indicated

	1999–2000 £	2000–2001 £
Attendance Allowance		
Higher rate	52.95	53.55
Lower rate	35.40	35.80
Child Benefit		
Elder or eldest qualifying child		
Couple	14.40	15.00
Lone parent	17.10	17.55
Each subsequent child	9.60	10.00
Special allowance	11.35	11.35
Council Tax Benefit		
Personal allowances		
Single, 18–24	40.70	41.35
Single, 25 plus	51.40	52.20
Lone parent, 18 plus	51.40	52.20
Couple, one or both over 18	80.65	81.95
Dependent children		
Birth–16	25.90	26.60
16–19	30.95	31.75
Disability Living Allowance		
Care component		
Highest	52.95	53.55
Middle	35.40	35.80
Lowest	14.05	14.20
Mobility component		
Higher	37.00	37.40
Lower	14.05	14.20
Earnings Rules		
Invalid care allowance	50.00	50.00
Therapeutic earnings limit	58.00	58.50
Industrial injuries earnings		
level (p.a.)	3016.00	3042.00
War pensioner's earnings		
level (p.a.)	3016.00	3042.00
Housing Benefit		
Personal allowances		
Single, 16–24	40.70	41.35
Single, 25 plus	51.40	52.20
Lone parent, under 18	40.70	41.35
18 plus	51.40	52.20
Couple, both under 18	61.35	62.35
One or both over 18	80.65	81.95
Birth–16	25.90	26.60
16–19	30.95	31.75
Incapacity Benefit		
Long-term	66.75	67.50
Short-term		
Under pension age		
Lower rate	50.35	50.90
Higher rate	59.55	60.20
Over pension age		
Lower rate	64.05	64.75
Higher rate	66.75	67.50
Increase of long-term incapacity		
benefit for age		
Higher rate	14.05	14.20
Lower rate	7.05	7.10
Invalidity allowance		
(transitional)		
Higher rate	14.05	14.20
Middle rate	8.90	9.00
Lower rate	4.45	4.50

	1999–2000 £	2000–2001 £
Income Support		
Personal allowances		
Single under 18, usual rate	30.95	31.45
18–24	40.70	41.35
25 plus	51.40	52.20
Lone parent under 18,		
usual rate	30.95	31.45
18 plus	51.40	52.20
Couple, both under 18	61.35	62.35
One or both 18 or over	80.65	81.95
Dependent children		
Birth–16	25.90	26.60
16–19	30.95	31.75
Residential allowance	59.40	61.30
Greater London	66.10	68.20
Premiums		
Family	13.90	14.25
Lone parent	15.75	15.90
Pensioner, single	23.60	26.25
Couple	35.95	40.00
Pensioner (enhanced) single	25.90	28.65
Couple	39.20	43.40
Pensioner (higher), single	30.85	33.85
Couple	44.65	49.10
Disability, single	21.90	22.25
Couple	31.25	31.75
Severe disability, single	39.75	40.20
Couple (one qualifies)	39.75	40.20
Disabled child	21.90	22.25
Carer	13.95	14.15
Max amounts for accommodation		
and meals in residential		
care homes		
Old age	218.00	221.00
Very dependent elderly	252.00	256.00
Mental disorder (not handicap)	230.00	234.00
Drug/alcohol dependence	230.00	234.00
Mental handicap	262.00	266.00
Physical disablement		
Under pension age	298.00	303.00
Over pension age	218.00	221.00
Industrial Death Benefit		
Widow's pension, higher rate	66.75	67.50
Lower rate	20.03	20.25
Industrial Injuries Disablement Pension		
18 plus or under 18 with dependents		
100 per cent	108.10	109.30
50 per cent	54.05	54.65
20 per cent	21.62	21.86
Invalid Care Allowance	39.95	40.40
Jobseekers Allowance		
Personal allowances		
Single, under 18, usual rate	30.95	31.45
Single, 18–24	40.70	41.35
Single, 25 or over	51.40	52.20
Couple, both under 18	30.95	31.45
Couple, both over 18	80.65	81.95
Maternity Allowance		
Lower	51.70	52.25
Higher	59.55	60.20
New standard rate	—	60.20
Retirement Pension		
Category A or B	66.75	67.50
Category B (lower)		
husband's insurance	39.95	40.40
Category C or D		
non-contributory	39.95	40.40
Category C (lower)		
non-contributory	23.90	24.15

Index

Accounts 26, 28, 100, 102
Accrued income securities 64
Additional personal
   allowance 5, 6, 44, 73, 139
Additional Voluntary
   Contributions (AVCs) 131
Adoption allowances 12
Age-related allowance 5, 72,
   91,
Allowance restriction 83
Allowances 5, 6, 41, 43, 59,
   72, 139
Annuities 11, 12, 14, 69, 96,
   97, 131
Assessments 86, 107
Attendance allowance 12

Bad debts 26, 101
Balance sheet 28
Bank interest 12, 61, 80, 94,
   101, 124
Basic rate of tax 5, 86, 139
Benefits 7, 11, 21, 55, 56, 84
Betting winnings 13, 114
Bicycles 54
Blind persons 5, 18, 43, 73,
   139
Bonds 64, 95, 127
Bonuses 12, 48
Bridging loans 68
Budget summary 5
Building society interest 12,
   39, 80, 94, 124
Business Expansion Scheme
   69, 114

Canteen facilities 55
Capital allowances, 8, 22, 27,
   31, 63, 105, 106
Capital Bonds 12, 64, 95
Capital gains 36, 113
   businesses 114, 119
   tax 8, 23, 36, 116, 139
   tax return 110
Capital gains retirement relief
   118
Car benefits 7, 21, 51, 111
Car expenses 26, 60, 102
Car parking 13

Cash basis 109
Casual work 11, 41, 48
Ceasing employment 79
Chargeable assets 118
Charities 70
   covenants 70, 130
   donations 130
   gift aid 70
   gifts 121
   legacies 120
Child benefit 13, 77
Child care 55, 77
Children's income 65, 77
Children's tax credit 9
Christmas bonus
   (pensioners) 13, 40
Clerical workers 59
Clerics 12
Clothing 56, 59, 101
Code number 15, 74, 81,
Commissions 11, 48
Compensation 11, 13, 22, 49,
   113
Computer Equipment 8, 56
Construction industry 9, 26,
   59
Contracting out 111
Corporate Venturing scheme
   10
Corporation tax 9, 139
Council tax 63
Covenants 42, 70, 130
Credit cards 21, 56, 69

Damages awards 13, 113
Death 78
Depreciation 26, 102
Directors 48, 61
Disabled 13, 14, 51
Disabled tax credit 6, 13, 140
Dispensation 61
Dividends 12, 33, 39, 64, 87
Divorce 78
Double taxation 33, 58

Education grants/awards 13,
   56
Employment abroad 11, 57
Employment tax return 20

Enterprise incentives 9
Enterprise Investment
   Schemes 42, 70, 114, 128
Entertaining 26, 102
Ex-gratia payments 13, 49
Expenses 11, 22, 30, 51, 59,
   101

Factory workers 59
Family credit 13
Family income supplement 13
Fees 12, 48, 60
Finance houses 127
First year allowances 106
Fixed profit car scheme 54
Foreign
   Income 22, 58
   tax return 32, 57
Form 33 15
Form 575 93
Form RU6 16
Free-Standing Additional
   Voluntary Contributions
   (FSAVC) 131
Freelance work 11, 41, 48
Friendly societies 41, 71
Fuel benefits 7, 21, 53, 56
Furnished accommodation 11,
   31

Gift aid 7, 43, 70
Gifts 7, 13, 60, 101, 114,
   121
Gilts 95, 114, 127
Government securities 95,
   114, 127
Gratuities 11, 49

Healthcare workers 59
Health schemes 21, 56, 69
Higher rate tax 6, 87, 139
Hire purchase 69, 102
Holiday benefit 56
Holiday pay 11
Home income schemes 6, 96
House 13, 60, 66, 114, 129
Housing benefit 13
Husbands 43, 62, 78, 104

Incapacity benefits 11, 13, 40
Incentive schemes 11
Income bonds 12, 95
Income support 13, 40
Indexation 115
Individual Learning Account 7, 66
Individual Savings Accounts (ISAs) 7, 13, 114, 126
Industrial death benefit 11, 40, 58
Industrial injury awards 13
Inflation 115
Inheritance tax 8, 69, 120, 139
Insurance 13, 41, 63, 100
Insurance bonds 13
Insurance premium tax 63
Interest
   paid 31, 55, 61, 63, 66, 68
   received 12, 13, 21, 33, 39, 63, 80
Invalid care allowance 11, 40, 58
Invalidity pension 13
Investments 68, 94, 124

Jobfinder's grant 13, 56
Jobseeker's allowance 11, 40, 48, 58

'Key' money 12

Land and property tax return 30
Legacies 120
Legal fees 26, 31, 63
Life policies 13, 41, 114
Living accommodation 21, 54, 56
Lloyds tax return 25
Loan interest 11, 55, 68
Long service awards 13
Losses 27, 29, 31, 108
Lottery winnings 13, 114
Luncheon vouchers 11, 56

Mail order commissions 11

Maintenance/alimony 6, 11, 12, 41, 65, 69
Manual workers 59
Married couples
   allowances 5, 6, 12, 43, 72, 75, 91, 139
   capital gains 114
   death of a husband/wife 78
   investments 62
   mortgage interest 67
   self-employed 99
   tax savings 76, 92
Maternity pay/allowance 14, 40, 58, 112
Mileage allowance 7, 21, 53
Millennium gift aid 8, 43, 71
Miners' coal allowance 14
Miras 67
Mobile telephones 54
Mortgage interest 6, 67, 129
Motorbikes 7, 54

National Insurance
   contributions 7, 28, 30, 74, 99, 110
National Savings 12, 13, 39, 64, 95, 96, 124
Non-residence 37
Notice of code 15, 81

Office workers 59
One-parent families see single parents
Overdue tax 89
Overseas employment 11, 33, 57
Overseas investment/property 12, 33

P2(T) form 15
P9D form 16
P11D form 16, 20, 55, 61
P38(S) form 78
P45 form 16, 20, 90, 100
P60 form 15, 20, 48, 84
Partnerships 29, 69, 100
Partnership tax return 25, 29
PAYE 8, 74, 81, 99

PAYE settlement agreement 61
Payment on account 47, 89
Payroll giving 8, 130
Penalties 47
Pension mortgages 129
Pension schemes 8, 42, 58, 69, 130
Pensioners 80, 90, 92
Pensioners Guaranteed Income Bonds 95
Pensions 12, 14, 45, 58, 90, 130
PEPs 14, 114, 125
Personal allowances 5, 72, 91, 139
PIBs 127
Plant and machinery 105
Pools winnings 13, 114
Post cessation 43, 109
Premium Bonds 14
Profit-related pay 7, 12, 14, 49
Profit-sharing 7, 57
Profits 12, 27, 29, 103
Property income and expenses 31, 62, 67, 129
Provident benefits 14

Quick succession relief 122

R40 form 15, 78, 94
R85 form 76, 94
Rates of tax 5, 115, 139
Redundancy 12, 14
Reliefs 41
Relocation 56
Rent rebates 14
Rent-a-room 14, 31, 63
Rents
   paid 63, 102
   received 12, 30, 63
Repairs 26, 101
Repayments 14, 45, 88, 89, 94
Research tax credits 106
Retirement 79, 90, 91
Retirement annuity 69, 97, 108, 119, 132

Retirement pension 12, 58, 97
Reverse premiums 12, 32
Royalties 12
RU6(M) form 16

SA300 statement 17, 89
SA302 notice 16, 88
SA303 form 89
Salaries 12, 21, 48
Salesmen 59
Savings 5, 63, 80, 86, 124
SAYE schemes 7, 14, 57, 114
Scrip dividends 12, 40, 64
Season tickets 56
Self assessment 16, 88, 133
Self-employed 9, 99, 109
 retirement relief 119
 tax return 25
Separation *see* Divorce
Settlements *see* Trust income
Share schemes 7, 14, 23, 57
Shares *see* Stocks and shares
Shop workers 59
Sickness benefits 14
Simplified accounts 105
Single parent 73, 75, 78
Small businesses 9, 123

Social Security 33, 45, 141
Stakeholder pensions 132
Stamp duty 9
Statement of account 89
Statutory sick pay 12, 40, 58, 112
Stipends 12
Stock dividends 12
Stocks and shares 23, 95, 127
Strike pay 14
Students 14, 78
Sub-contractors 28
Subscriptions 22, 60, 101
Surcharges 47

Tapering relief 115
Tax computation 85, 100, 102
Tax credits 39, 87, 92
Tax refunds 15, 45, 79, 89, 94, 95
Tax return 15, 18, 47
Telephone 60, 101
TESSAs 14, 114, 125
Tips 11, 49
Trade unions 59, 71
Transitional allowance 43
Transport benefits 7
Travelling expenses 22, 26, 53, 59, 60

Trust income 12, 35, 64

Unemployed 75, 79
Unemployed benefits 14, 40, 58
Unit trusts 127

Vans 21, 53, 106
VAT 9, 100, 139
Venture Capital Trusts 14, 42, 70, 114, 128
Vocational training 7, 66

Wages 12, 21, 31, 48
War widow's benefit 14
Widowed mother's allowance 12, 40
Widow's allowance/pension 12, 40, 73
Widow's bereavement allowance 5, 6, 44, 139
Widow's payment 14
Wills 79, 123
Winter fuel payment 14
Wives 43, 62, 78, 104
Working families tax credit 6, 14, 75, 140
Writing down allowance 106